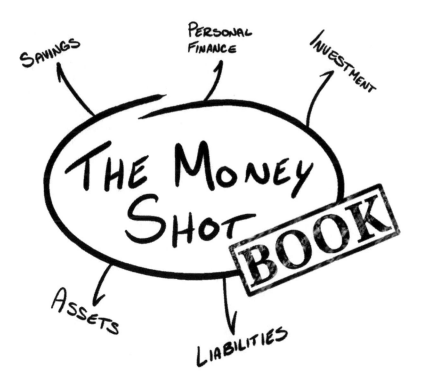

THE [**SLIGHTLY LESS DULL**] GUIDE TO
PERSONAL FINANCE AND INVESTING

DAMIEN FOGG

Let's Tell Your Story
London

COPYRIGHT

Title: The Money Shot: The (Slightly Less Dull) Guide to Personal Finance and Investing

First published in 2018 by Let's Tell Your Story Publishing

Address: 5 Century Court, Tolpit's Lane, Watford, WD18 9RS

ISBN: 978-1-910600-22-1

Illustrations: Hrefna Bragadottir

Book design: Colette Mason

Editing: Greg Fidgeon

DISCLAIMER

This book has been prepared solely for informational (and a little bit entertainmental) purposes and is not an offer to buy or sell or a solicitation of an offer to buy or sell any security, product, service or investment. Nor does it constitute any form of personal recommendation.

Basically – don't read this and then think you know it all, buy something stupid and then come blame me for it. Speak to a professional who knows your complete and individual circumstances.

I, and the publisher, make no warranty, expressed or implied, about the accuracy or reliability of the information in this book or any resource mentioned or linked to the book. The information is provided for education and guidance only.

Wow, reading that makes no sense. I think I've just said everything I've written is bollocks? Thanks disclaimer people.

Past performance is not a guide to future performance. Investments can go down as well as up and you may end up losing money if you invest in some of the assets mentioned in this book.

Look, investments are hard. Professionals get it wrong a lot. Like, a lot, a lot. So reading a book, as great as this one is, isn't going to make you an investing god or goddess. You'll make a mess at some point. I just don't want you blaming me for it!

So, take whatever it is you need to from this and do your own research – always – before investing.

Special mention goes to my folks for everything they have done.

Kids. Expensive investments, but hopefully one that has paid dividends.
(I'm such a finance nerd, I can't help it!)

CONTENTS

ACKNOWLEDGEMENTS

Apparently, this is where I'm meant to thank everyone I've ever spoken to about anything. Ever.

I've already dedicated the book to my folks, so they can do one.

Suppose I should thank my publisher Colette for literally dragging this book out of me and turning the ramblings of a ranting money-obsessed nutter into what you're reading now.

Greg Figdeon rocked up with this editorial red pen and wrote all over my first draft. It was utter carnage, but it's made it better for you, dear reader, so that's alright then.

Jon Buchan tried to make my quips funnier, I suppose. "Tried" being the operative word. Let's face it, it's finance, FFS, so it was bound to be a tough gig.

My artistic ability starts and ends with scrawling notes on a whiteboard, so mercfully, Hrefna Bragadottir added the illustrations, to create some visual interest to stop you slipping into unconsciousness when "living within your means" was punted about as an idea.

And I should also thank a bunch of other people too, probably. But I can't remember you now, so I guess you weren't that helpful.

INTRODUCTION

About Me

Hello. I'm Damien Fogg. I'm guessing you knew that by now.

I'm usually described as a "loveable little shit". I don't know where people get the loveable part from.

You know how when you're younger you want to grow up to be a racing driver or an astronaut or a Vegas showgirl (for the disturbed among you)? Well, when I was knee-high to a grasshopper I wanted to be a financial adviser.

What can I say? I'm a rebellious maverick. When other teenagers were hiding their cigarettes, I was hiding my copy of Securities Analysis by Benjamin Graham (it's an absolute laugh riot, I promise you).

Anyway, I went down that route for a while and then realised it was mostly filling out forms and who has time for that shit? So I did a bunch of other stuff instead.

Snowboard instructor, personal trainer, day trader, financial adviser, copywriter, distributor.

Having grown up reading the FT on the weekends, my love of money and numbers has never left me. I realised the thrill of snowboarding would never match the excitement I found in the world of property investment or, more accurately, the pay.

And because I'm a mega-nerd, I got a master's degree in it. Then I got chartered as a building surveyor, and then consulted with the EU, the National Landlords Association and the Homes & Communities Agency.

I'm kind of a big deal.

But I'm also a tumbling dickweed.

So instead of doing all the professional grown-up things, I just started working with people who I like and who I can help mimic what I did.

And that was to retire in my early 30s due to the passive income I had built up. Don't get me wrong, I wasn't a zillionaire or anything, but the money that came in from my investments was enough to cover my outgoings.

Sounds cool, right?

WHY I WROTE THIS BOOK

It's great working closely with people I like. I get to hang out with awesome guys and gals and talk about a topic I'm disturbingly obsessed with while helping them out at the same time.

But often the conversation turns away from property investment and gets into general personal finance and investing.

It turns out that not everyone grew up reading the Sunday Times Money section and asking how gross redemption yields are influenced by the base rate of interest. Who'd have thought it?

So I wrote this book for two reasons.

First, to help show you how easy finances and investing can be once you get rid of the douchebags that usually talk about it.

And second, I can now just throw this book at the next person who asks me, "So where should I start?" or "Have you ever thought about writing a book on personal finance?".

Who This Book Is For

I'm writing this book for you.

It is for someone who is ready to take control of their finances and start investing but don't really know how to track their finances, or how to come up with a simple plan to follow, or even what is possible to invest in.

You know that you should probably start doing something to plan for the future.

However, you know you don't want to sacrifice having fun in the meantime. Putting all your money into a boring, long-term investment portfolio sounds like a shitty idea.

This book aims to help you find the happy middle ground where you can have a safe and secure future but still enjoy the now.

That's who this book's for.

WHAT THIS BOOK COVERS

The mind-numbingly monotonous world of investing. Woohoo!

But, instead of making you want to gouge out your eyes with a spoon, I'm aiming to make you inappropriately excited about how simple it can be to be the master of your own financial destiny.

At least that's the plan. I take zero responsibility for any loss of eyes due to the content of this book.

It's broken up into three main sections.

The first covers the Fundamental Principles. Master these and you'll be ahead of 90 per cent of the population when it comes to financial intelligence. Balls them up and you're screwed.

Specifically, we will look at what living within your means actually means and how to achieve it. This is the cornerstone of your financial success. You will learn why you need to take control of your money so you are able to create a plan for it to help you in the future without sacrificing the now (yes, you are still allowed a few nights out, but maybe not on the Dom Perignon all the time).

We'll also get into some technical stuff such as compounding and pounding, which is the basis of understanding how to get your money working harder for you. And there's a warning too, on avoiding the snake-oil salesman.

In Section 2 we'll cover the Basic Principles. This is the practical stuff you can use to take full control of your finances and come up with a detailed and specific plan for yourself.

We'll look in detail at how to track your incomings and outgoings – and why it's important to do so – as well as how to increase them or reduce them accordingly. You'll also learn what assets and liabilities are, how to measure them and why not all liabilities are bad. It concludes with us working out a figure that will be your dream income. Nice.

In the third section – Assets and Portfolios – we get into the nitty-gritty of what you can actually invest in so you can work out if it's for you or not.

We take a look at all the different types of assets including equities/shares, funds, bonds, currencies, commodities, properties, cash, cryptocurrencies, and alternatives (I know, all this financial talk is making you feel all sexy, right?). I will tell you the pros and cons of each, the risk-to-reward ratio, the time horizon for each and the minimum financial commitments needed.

And we finish off by examining how – when you are at that stage financially – to split your money across different asset classes, choosing the best asset allocation portfolio for you, checking your net worth and rebalancing your assets to keep you on track for the next 20, 40 or 100 years.

By the time you get to the end of this section, you should be able to confidently stride into the world of investments and towards your financial security. Well, at least be better placed to do so than before you read the book. Hopefully.

How To Use The Book

You should read this book from start to finish and don't cherry-pick bits and pieces as you go along.

You need to go through each level to progress to the next one. There's no point jumping to the end if you haven't sorted out the stuff at the start. Things will unravel quickly if you do that, trust me.

Complete the quizzes at the end of each section to ensure you haven't drifted off into a boredom-induced coma. If the info you have read hasn't sunk in, and if you aren't putting it into action, then the chances are that the next chapter won't help you too much either.

I've tried to keep it entertaining but some of the topics might be hard going. I am not a miracle worker; it is finance after all.

As always with a finance book, I need to do one of those big fat disclaimers shouted from the rooftops by some bloke dressed up like a biscuit-tin character: "Be ye warned. This be not financiale advyce."

I appreciate this can sound a bit dickish and like I'm trying to get out of any responsibility, but there genuinely is a good reason for it.

Imagine I came to you and said I wanted you to organise a party for me on Saturday. And that's all I told you. It would be pretty hard to nail that request when you don't even know:

- Why you are having the party
- Who is coming
- Where the venue is

- What music everyone likes
- If people need feeding
- If people need alcoholing
- Are the Backstreet Boys still cool (Yes... Yes they are)

If I asked you to do that, then maybe 20 per cent of the time the result would be close enough and we'd have kind of a good party. Five per cent of the time (if I'm being generous) it'd be legendary and you'd get everything just right.

But without any of that information, it's pure guesswork and blind luck that you get it spot on.

That's why a book isn't specialised advice designed just for you. I just don't have enough details to tailor anything to you.

Much like a travel guidebook talks about the wonders (and draw-backs) of city, beach and mountain adventures, it's on you to go and research your holiday in more depth to figure out what's the right destination for you.

If we're both lucky, this will be a slightly less dreary introduction to a topic filled with boring personalities and dry facts and figures.

Sticking with the holiday theme, think of this book as the slightly dodgy 18-30 rep on a Greek island that you regrettably sleep with halfway through the trip but who showed you all the cool places. I'm that person, rather than the retired historian giving a walking tour around Rotherham. (Sorry to those of you from Rotherham. I've never even been, but your town just sounds dull).

But anyway, I'm bored of this section now, so bonus points if you made it here. Let's crack on.

Resources

I've put a net worth sheet together for you [*Hang on Damien, you've sneaked some blooming jargon in already, FFS! – Ed*] which will allow you to take complete ownership of your finances.

You'll be able to see how much is coming in, how much is going out, what you own, what you owe, and where you want to get to. It's all on one simple sheet.

I've also put together some questions that you can ask any financial adviser just to make sure you're speaking to the right person and not somebody who is 12 years old and doesn't have a clue (or any money themselves), or who is just trying to flog you the crap that pays the highest commission, so they can buy another shiny suit and get their teeth whitened. Again.

Keep In Touch

The good news for you is that I don't bite, often or hard. At least I don't draw blood – huzzah! So feel free to get in touch with me.

Drop me an email if you like: damien@theEPinvestor.com

I have a fun-filled, free Facebook group – The EP Investor Group (https://www.facebook.com/groups/theepinvestor) that you're more than welcome to join and ask any questions you might have.

Ideally, these will be investment-based questions and not stupid stuff like, "Where did I leave my keys?" or depressing shit such as,

"Why does my partner no longer look me in the eyes during sex?".
If it's not that kind of question, then ask away.

Of course, I'll have a pop at answering the above should you ask,
but I'm not sure I'll have a good answer for you.

The last place you left them? Probably in the kitchen. On the side.
You forgot to put them back in the right place after you brought
the shopping in.

Because your "arrival" face reminds them of an endangered sea
creature, and it makes it hard to think of the cute guy/gal from the
local chippy while looking at that.

See, told you I wouldn't have good answers.

For some reason, we still see finances as a dirty topic in the UK, so
if you want to chat privately then feel free to get in touch and we
can chat one to one.

SECTION 1

FUNDAMENTAL PRINCIPALS

"Money is only a tool. It will take you wherever
you wish, but it will not replace you as the driver"

Ayn Rand

Before we delve into the fascinating and mysterious world of the fundamentals of personal finance, let me ask you a question.

Let's imagine you've just found £1,000 lying around somewhere. Down the back of the couch maybe or in a jeans pocket (are you a drug dealer?). Wherever it came from, it doesn't really matter. It's a nice little cheeky surprise. In financial terms that's a "windfall" (See, I'm teaching you shit already).

And now you've got to decide what to do with that glorious cold, hard cash. So what's the first thing you'd do with it?

Go ahead, take your time and be honest with yourself. What would you do with this new windfall?

I bet you've imagined a few things already.

Are you going to buy some new pricey-but-you're-worth-it face cream?

How about screaming with glee at the top of your voice on a roller-coaster whizzing round at Alton Towers theme park?

Are you going to treat someone you love to something delightful like a freshly baked sausage roll or, I don't know, a fancy new watch or handbag?

Maybe a holiday or some exercise equipment that you'll no doubt use all the time? Or one of those helicopter experience days?

What is it you're going to do with that filthy lucre?

Anyone in the class going to be a grown-up and think about investing it in something dull and boring?

Anybody? Anybody? Bueller? Anybody?

Well, I'm sat here writing a book aimed at making you more fiscally responsible, putting you on a path of long-term financial prudence so you can build the perfect life for you and your family and I'm leaning more towards doing something daft. That helicopter ride sounds Dreamy McDreamerson.

Luckily for you, I like you enough to finish this book. I'm nice like that. That and my editor terrifies me, so I have no choice.

With no further ado, let me proudly introduce Fundamental Principle #1.

FUNDAMENTAL PRINCIPLE #1
LIVE WITHIN YOUR MEANS

If you can't live within your means then you're on a slippery slope to ending up poor. That's if things pan out well, but if you really screw it up you'll be bankrupt.

When you live within your means you will have surplus money at the end of each month and year that is going to allow you to save and invest. It will also allow you to keep and build your nest egg, as big or as small as it might be.

It will mean you don't have to dip into your savings to fund your lavish lifestyle.

Think about celebrities that end up going bankrupt. They're earning a lot but they're not living within their means. Before they know it, they're bankrupt and desperately trying to figure out how they got into such a mess while frantically putting their beloved pet tiger on eBay.

My point is this: By living within your means you'll have more options available. Alas, you have to forgo the little things in life like diamond-encrusted teeth and keeping enormous endangered cats as pets.

So how do you live within your means? In the short term, it's important to check frequently how you're doing financially – not just at the end of each month. You need to be checking whether you spend more than you earn and where the money actually goes? You need to be monitoring your incomings and outgoings in real-time including all those poncey coffees you're buying, those takeaways you order and even that Amazon Prime habit you've got (1-click purchase is the work of the devil). It's time to be a bit more proactive in budgeting and know where your money's going.

Think about the big, expected incomings that you've got. Maybe that's an annual bonus or a large dividend from a company.

Also, think about the large expected and known outgoings. It could be the annual car service on the rust bucket you own or the house insurance on your property. These things you know about in advance and can proactively budget for. For some people, even simple things like paying with cash rather than using credit cards can make spending a little more conscious and really drive home the question of whether you really do need to buy that beautiful new backpack that's been begging you to give it a new home.

Longer term, there are really two ways to live within your means. You can either increase your incomings so that you can afford the lavish lifestyle to which you've become accustomed or you can decrease your outgoings so that you live within the incomings that you currently have. Personally, I'm a fan of combining the two. Kinky, I know.

You don't need to live an overly frugal lifestyle and avoid the daily coffees if that's what you like. But making sure you spend the money on stuff that has a real positive impact on your life is where it's at. Not just buying the coffee out of habit or because you fancy the person on the checkout. Just ask them out already! See, you're even getting some free dating advice. Don't worry, I promise to stick to financial advice for the remainder of this book.

You can also plan for some things. For purchases such as mobile phones, you can consider whether to pay upfront for the phone and have a lower monthly commitment, or whether to spread the cost over two years and have a higher bill each month.

There is no right or wrong answer here, but simply being aware of these decisions and what impact they have on your finances is important.

Living within your means is going to make you more conscious of what is the right decision for you.

FUNDAMENTAL PRINCIPLE #2
PAY YOURSELF FIRST

It's been a long-held belief in the financial world that you should pay yourself first (and invest or save the money) before you pay for anything else.

But that's a bit impractical. Really this bit should be called "Pay yourself second". I think it's important to inject an element of reality into ideal finances and how we all live. The most important principle here, though, is that it's very easy to slip into having no plan at all. So the sooner you can start getting into the habit of paying yourself first, or second in this case, the better.

In practice, this means taking a set percentage of your income and immediately transferring it into a savings or investment account.

Frivolous spending is not conscious spending. It's very easy if the money is just sat there staring at you – and you don't have a plan for it – to treat yourself or go out for a night on the town with your mates.

Remember that £1,000 windfall from earlier? If you had a plan in place for additional money then you would have known exactly what to do with it then and there – and not be stumbling around on your new high heels already.

You're much less likely to save if you're not measuring and don't have a plan in place. When I say pay yourself second, really the first thing you need to do is cover your absolute basic needs. Things like your house, food and paying off debts. These should be your top priorities. It's kind of important to have somewhere to live and it's quite nice to eat.

Once you've covered those bare essentials – and what counts as essential is going to change for each individual – and before you spend your money on anything else, you should set aside a percentage of your incomings towards saving and investing.

Usually, the advice is 10 per cent and for a lot of people 10 per cent is very doable. For others, it could be five per cent or 50.

The point is to have a specific plan and stick to it. Immediately transferring the money out of your spending account into another savings or investment account is hugely important and a great habit to get into.

For entrepreneurs or self-employed people, you have to bear in mind the fact that taxes are kind of a thing. It makes sense to set aside 20 per cent of the revenue coming in for tax purposes.

I know there are far more fun ways to spend your money. I love drinking, partying and helicopter trips as much as the next man. However, saving in advance beats having a huge tax bill land on your desk as you panic to figure out how you'll pay it.

There is a trade-off to be had between securing the future and having fun now. I'm the last person to judge when it comes to spending money on stupid shit:

- £500 on full fencing gear, but quit fencing the next day
- £1,500 on camera equipment, but don't like carrying camera equipment around with me so never take a picture

- £900 on air assault bike, but it spends 60 per cent of its time being a clothes rack
- £2,000 on a piano, but only had three lessons

I buy stupid shit from the internet all the time. I swear, if I had a dollar for every time I purchased some stupid shit from the internet, I'd probably use the money to purchase more stupid shit from the internet.

The stupid purchases I've mentioned above are "allowed" because I made them after having already stuck to my first few rules.

I'm not telling you to stop being an idiot; I'm telling you to become a savvier idiot. I know that's a lofty goal, but with hard work and effort, you can get there.

Don't just spend your money because you can, spend it on things you really want. Make conscious decisions about what you should spend your cash on and if there's nothing that really grabs you or adds pleasure to your life then maybe top up your savings for the month.

Always reacting at the end of the month and not having a plan in place will inevitably lead to long-term disappointment.

FUNDAMENTAL PRINCIPLE #3
PLAN FOR THE FUTURE, BUT ENJOY THE NOW

So far everything's been terribly grown-up and responsible, but it's important that you don't go too far with your frugality and minimalism and end up living in a cave like a hermit.

You can't take money with you when you pop your clogs – it's basically there to give you options and buy happiness in life.

That whole money doesn't buy happiness thing? It's bollocks. It was either said by someone poor, by someone rich who didn't want you to get rich or by someone who's never invested in a quality backpack collection.

My money, as you may have guessed, helps me to fund my spiralling backpack habit. I really did need two this week, honestly. One is for day trips and the other for three-day trips. And they complement my backpacks for five and seven-day trips. There are so many pockets on all of them!

There is a balance to be had here. While it's important to think about the future and plan how you'll make it a comfortable one, you don't want to compromise your now so that it's so boring you're not even looking forward to the future anymore.

Equally, you don't want to go the other way and spend your money on absolutely everything on the basis that you never know when you'll be hit by the proverbial bus. What if you're unlucky and you don't get hit by a bus? Now you're going to end up broke, old and too frail to throw yourself in front of the next double-decker that comes along.

If you keep the balance somewhere in the middle then you could end up having a good now and a good future. It's very hard to catch up later in life if you've already spunked all your cash on stupid stuff while you're younger.

Equally, if you've been saving for your future the whole time and you die young, it's a bit of a waste to leave all that money to the donkey sanctuary. Just sayin'. (My Mam's obsessed with donkey sanctuaries, I don't know why).

FUNDAMENTAL PRINCIPLE #4
COMPOUNDING AND POUNDING

This is slightly technical, but it's kind of a big deal. Stick with me here and I promise to reward you with the lamest joke I know.

Compounding means the sooner you start, the easier it is for you to magic up money out of thin air. Sounds quite cool when you put it like that. Your pounds will reproduce the longer you can have them invested and working on your behalf.

It's a bit like a family that has two kids and then those two kids each have two kids, and those four grandkids each have two kids, and those eight great-grandkids each have two kids, and so on, and so on. You get the picture. Not that they could all fit in one picture.

After a few generations, there are hundreds of the little buggers.

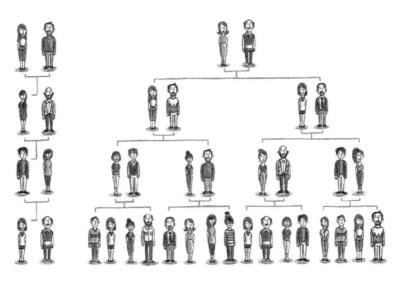

Now compare that to the family that has one kid, and their kid has one kid, and their kid has one kid, etc. In fact, screw it; here's a diagram to break up the text and to give you something fun to look at.

As you can see, both started off with the same number of units. But one family grew just a little bit more each time until there were eventually more of them than grains of sand on a beach.

I imagine, at some point, they probably ate the other family. Probably. I dunno why.

You're pretty smart so I'm sure you can see how this relates to money. But if not; let me explain. When you invest your money and it grows, you now have a bit more invested that can grow again. And when that grows there is even more money to grow.

That £1,000 growing at five per cent becomes £1,050, which then becomes £1,102.50, which then becomes £1,157.63 and then £1,215.51 and then £1,276.28, etc. It grows exponentially (that just means quicker and quicker each time). If you leave it alone for a while and let it keep on keeping on, it goes mental.

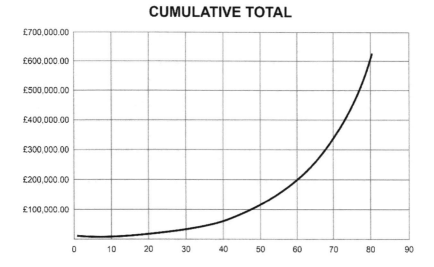

CUMULATIVE TOTAL

Fun, but not that exciting, huh? OK, well how about we add in Pound Cost Averaging as well then?

Pound Cost Averaging refers to buying more of something on a regular basis. As an example, we'll say you buy a coffee every day on your way to work. Sometimes it's from Costa, sometimes from Fancy Italian Twattery Coffee Co and sometimes a flask of instant from your own cupboard.

Let's say it costs £2.20 from Costa, £3.50 from Twattery and £0.25 from home. You normally go to Costa twice a week, Twattery twice a week and homebrew once a week.

So you will spend £2.20, £3.50, £2.20, £0.25 and £3.50 over the course of the week. In all, you get five coffees over the course of the week and it costs £11.65 in total.

That's £2.33 per day on coffee on average. You madman! Now, let's see how Pound Cost Averaging helps.

Let's say you can buy fractions of a cup of coffee in these places (just go with me here). And instead of buying a single coffee, you're just going to buy £2.33 worth each day at the same places.

- Monday: £2.33 in Costa buys you 1.06 of a coffee
- Tuesday: £2.33 in Twattery buys you 0.66 of a coffee
- Wednesday: Back at Costa for 1.06 of a coffee
- Thursday: Oh crap! That £2.33 on homebrew gets you 9.32 cups of coffee
- Friday: Assuming you didn't die from yesterday's intake, you get another 0.66 of a coffee from Twattery

You will have spent exactly the same amount of money on coffee as you did in previous weeks, but now instead of getting five cups, you can have 12.76.

How? What is this magic of which I speak?

You bought fewer cups when it was expensive, but more when it was cheap.

(Now seems a good moment to admit I hate coffee. I don't like the smell of it, the taste of it or the look of it. But I would like to spend money on all the random accessories you can buy for it. I digress.)

If we translate this into finance then if, for example, you're buying shares of a company, you can use this method to buy fewer shares when the share price is really high and more when the price is low.

You no longer have to worry about timing the market. You can just set up a simple payment plan to buy consistently at regular intervals and end up with a much better outcome than if you tried instead to buy one share every month.

To give you another example, let me tell you about Sensible Steve and Dickhead Pete.

Sensible Steve has invested 10 per cent of his income into a balanced portfolio every month since he first started work.

When prices were low, he invested 10 per cent of his income and bought a crap-load of units. When prices were high he still invested the same 10 per cent of his income but now was buying fewer units. He did this for years.

Whenever he got a pay rise, the amount he invested each month increased, but remained consistent at 10 per cent of his income.

Now he's in his 40s, he has built a portfolio that's in the hundreds of thousands and has a property portfolio that can cover his costs for the rest of his life.

Now, look at Dickhead Pete. He spent his money like it was going out of fashion. He had a new car every couple of years, a holiday every six months, etc. Nothing ridiculous, but he didn't have a savings plan and wasn't investing along the way.

He's the same age and has the same kind of profession as Sensible Steve, but has a different mentality when it comes to investing.

One is effectively retired and now chooses to work a three-day week so he's got something to do. The other works five days a week and is freaking out about his retirement as he hasn't got anything set aside for it and is looking down the barrel of another 30 years of working.

It's time for you to make a decision. A decision that will have a bearing on your finances for the rest of your life. Who do you want to be? Sensible Steve or Dickhead Pete?

Oh, and I promised you the lamest joke ever.

What do you call Postman Pat when he retires?

Pat.

FUNDAMENTAL PRINCIPLE #5
NO SUCH THING AS A FREE LUNCH, IT'S TOO GOOD TO BE TRUE

If it looks too good to be true, it probably is. So don't be a greedy mug. Everyone's going to try and sell you something amazing, especially the snake-oil salesman.

Be wary of something that sounds absolutely amazing. Those sure-fire winners are probably not as great an opportunity as they are being sold to you.

The fact that other people are selling it hard has to make you think, 'Why aren't they just doing it themselves? Why are they banging on at me trying to sell it?'

Keep these thoughts in your head when you're assessing something that looks a little too good.

The buy-to-let market is a good example. When that was all kicking off in the mid-2000s everybody was selling the dream of unlimited potential and no money down and below market value – all these things.

It sounded great. Couldn't go wrong, right? You could buy a house that would go up by 20 per cent within a year and you didn't have to use any of your own money. Ace!

Eventually, though, it ended up causing a lot of people to go bankrupt when they were left with houses that couldn't be rented out for enough to cover the cost of the massive mortgages.

If you look overseas at the Bernie Madoff Ponzi scheme, people were giving him money because he had a fantastic record and the numbers he was producing looked amazing. But the only way he could do that was by being a massive fraud.

Keep your eyes open. If something looks too good to be true then do your due diligence and do it again before making a decision.

CLOSE

You should now be in a position to understand what living within your means actually means and have a good idea of how to do it.

You should also understand the importance of paying yourself first, or second. You're going to know how to plan for the future, but bear in mind you want to enjoy yourself along the way.

You understand the technical side of pounding and compounding, and how they can really benefit you by getting started investing sooner rather than later.

And, hopefully, I've helped you avoid some of the dodgier schemes out there by understanding that there's no such thing as a free lunch and that you need to review anything that looks a bit too good to be true. Twice.

Before we move onto the next stage I want you to answer that initial question again. What do you want to spend that £1,000 on?

Will you give the same answer or a different one now? Sensible or Dickhead? Don't answer immediately. Have a think. Choose wisely.

QUIZ

1) A Geography teacher is offered a new job and they are trying to decide what to do. Help them out. Should they:
   a) Stay in their current job earning £26,000 a year teaching kids in Sunderland how to find Scotland on a map while spending £23,000 a year on expenses?
   b) Move to Dubai and earn £62,000 a year teaching rich assholes what country they rule, but spend £82,000 a year on expenses?

1. Uncle Jimbo had a bumper month and brought home £5,000 from his various nefarious dealings. Oddly he has been paid at the beginning of the month (mostly because it makes this question easier), but he's trying to figure out what to do with his cash. Should he:
   a) Allocate his monthly expenses budget and set that aside first, before seeing what's left over for fun stuff to spend his money on?
   b) Buy a python costing £4,750 and assume more money will come in soon to pay for boring stuff like rent and bills?
   c) Invest £5,000 into Premium Bonds and hope he wins the £1million jackpot soon?

2. Would you rather have £1,000 that will increase by one per cent per day for the next two years or £500,000 cash now?
   a) £1,000 compounding, please.
   b) £500,000 cash.

3. I have some magic beans for sale. Will you buy them from me for £2,500? They are magic though and will earn you £8million within the next four weeks without any effort on your part.
   c) Sign me up!
   d) Hard pass.

SECTION 2

BASIC

PRINCIPLES

"Too many people spend money they haven't earned to buy things they don't want to impress people they don't like"

Will Smith

You were subjected to death by theory a little in that last section, so let's change things up and cover the more practical side of things.

We are going to look at how you get from where you are now to where you need to be – and how to keep track of your progress along the journey.

Sound good? Let's take a look.

BASIC PRINCIPLE #1
TRACK YOUR INCOMINGS

Incomings are the money that you get each month or year. It's the cash that comes from doing grown-up stuff like a job. Or it could be random things like babysitting, tutoring people or sucking off sailors down the docks. I'm not here to judge, babysitting is nothing to be ashamed of. But incomings can be any regular payment that you get.

It may be a six-monthly dividend or an annual bonus from your job. It doesn't matter where it comes from, but anything that comes in is considered income.

Why does all this matter? Well, it turns out that you need money to buy things. Life is quite expensive and most shit isn't free.

Your incomings are what you spend to buy stuff and things. (I told you this investment lark is quite easy, even when I'm using all these technical terms).

You need to be fully aware of what your income is on a monthly, quarterly and yearly basis so you can start planning.

HOW TO TRACK YOUR INCOMINGS

You're going to review 12 months of bank statements. (I saw that. Don't roll your eyes. Just get on with it).

Simply download these from your bank in an Excel format as that'll save you a bit of time. If you don't like computers that much, it's fine.

Just get a pen and paper out and write down everything that has gone into your bank account over that period.

It's a ball-ache, but once you've done it this first time it'll get much easier. I promise.

When you look at your bank statements there are going to be the total monthly incomings and outgoings for that time period at the top (usually on the right, but who knows?).

If you have a job and no other additional sources of income then that figure will probably do just fine and this process will take about three minutes.

For everyone else, look at the deposits column that shows the incoming money and see where it's come from.

Is it a one-off payment or is it a regular amount that's coming in? And how much is it? What you're looking for here are regular incoming payments and understanding where they come from.

For a lot of people, it will be a monthly salary and maybe an annual bonus, which is nice. You might also get monthly dividend payments from somewhere. This part is just figuring out where these things have come from and it is going to give you an idea of what you've earned over the last 12 months.

But everyone should review a full year just in case there are annual payments that you have forgotten about or missed.

There's no real point in going further back than a year – or two at most – because life does change over time. You may have got new kids or a new car or house or somehow been awarded a massive and undeserved raise out of nowhere. Things change.

Those are probably things you'd remember without having to be reminded by your bank statement, but it does mean your incomings may have changed so you're not really comparing apples with apples anymore.

As a side note for all you entrepreneurs reading this, I'm going to give you the benefit of the doubt and assume you do this already for your business, right? If not, guess what? You get to do all of this twice.

Yay!

How You Can Boost Your Income

Once you've looked at your incomings from the past 12 months you should then consider where it came from and what you did to earn it. Is it something you can do again?

If you were babysitting or tutoring someone, maybe it's a task you can repeat and earn more.

You should also look at other potential streams of income. If you're really good at your job, there's a good chance you can be paid to teach somebody else the same skills.

Working online as a virtual assistant is an option available to virtually everyone, but you'll get paid more if you have a specific skill you can share and teach others. Just think outside the box a little bit on that one.

You could also have a clear-out at home and see if there is anything you can sell. You have to be honest with yourself with this. Take a look at all the possessions you've amassed and ask the big, tough questions like, 'Do I really need that £900 Air Assault bike I'm using as a clothes horse?'

Another option might be to rent out a room in your house. That's going to bring in income each month for something that you've already got.

Or, finally, you can look at setting up your own side business. Maybe it is a dog-walking service or becoming an eBay or Amazon trader. There are any number of side businesses you can create and I've got a great resource for you if that's something you're considering. Check out the resource page at www.theEPinvestor.com/book

Just a warning reminder on that though: If the shiny and exciting offer you've stumbled upon looks too good to be true, remember our

Fundamental Principle #5 and don't get scammed by some douche-canoe with a rented Ferrari.

If all this income generation malarkey sounds like a bit of a pain in the arse, the other option is to control your outgoings or "tighten your belt" as your Granddad might have said.

And that's what we're going to look at next.

BASIC PRINCIPLE #2
Track your outgoings

Your outgoings are the money spent each month on everything. You can break that down to the essentials, the discretionary, and the bat-shit ridiculous (that's often thought of as the cool stuff).

You need to know how much money you're spending to be able to save some. It's the same as with your income, you can't plan properly if you don't know what those outgoings are.

You also need to know what categories your spending falls into as that will influence the decisions you need to make about them.

Finally, you should look at the benefits those outgoings are giving you. As we talked about previously, money is just there to give you options and make you happy. So if it's not doing those things, then do you really need to be throwing money at it?

The essentials are going to be things like food, shelter, clothing and travelling to your place of work.

Discretionary stuff is going to be things like a cinema pass for someone who's obsessed with films or date night to a decent restaurant with your better half. It's stuff that you don't really need, but you get quite a lot of benefit and enjoyment from.

And then there's the bat-shit ridiculous. That's your diamond-encrusted phone cases, the second expensive Rolex watch (the sort that's going to make you want to run when you find yourself down a dark alleyway), your umpteenth backpack, that second sports car that's a bit too low for someone of your age and waistline. It could be the most expensive bottle of wine on the menu that you bought to impress your date because it turns out she doesn't share your love of backpacks.

I don't understand women.

How To Measure Your Outgoings

This process is similar to that for your incomings, so I hope you've still got those bank statements handy.

Look for all of the standing orders and direct debits you have. There will be things such as your rent or mortgage, your utility bills, etc. These are your essentials, but your discretionary spending should also be on here.

Look at everything and then you can question whether it is worth the money. Do you genuinely use your Netflix every month or should you really be working on your side hustle?

Are there other regular payments going out that made sense at the time, but you probably don't need anymore or make you think, 'What the fuck was I thinking when I bought that?'

Do you really still need that luxury gym membership when you haven't been there since the times when connecting to the internet meant hearing a series of funny bings, pings and fuzzes?

After you've categorised each standing order and direct debit you can move on to all the other shit that's on your outgoings.

Look at the card payments you're making. Look at the cash you're withdrawing and frittering away on small day-to-day things. It's very easy to spend cash when it's just sat there in your pocket waiting to be spent.

Put all the expenses and the outgoings into very simple categories so that you can at least spot some of the patterns.

Maybe you spend all of your time going to fancy restaurants or you notice you buy an awful lot of takeaways.

Start batching them into groups so you can see where a lot of your money is going.

How To Reduce Your Outgoings

The first thing to consider is how easy it is to get rid of the cost. Can you get out of it immediately or are you tied into a contract or sub-scription? Maybe you should cancel or look at not renewing when the time comes.

The key thing here is to have some good, old-fashioned self-discipline. It's all on you.

Can You Reduce It?

The biggest step you can take with this is moving to a smaller property. Do you really need to live where you're living?

I know a lot of people won't raise this, but I promised I'd be honest with you – and aggressively friendly – so if you're serious about getting financial independence and all that jazz, then you've got to seriously look at the largest expense on your list and consider if you really need to live where you do now.

Slightly smaller steps could be things like taking packed lunches into work (hahaha, lunchbox wanker!) instead of buying food out, or taking your own cup to the coffee shop. I've just found out you pay less for not using their cups, mostly because the cost of the cup is the most expensive raw material in your coffee. Who knew?

Keep in mind the fact you don't want to live like a monk, so if you actually quite enjoy going out for lunch or buying that coffee then crack on. Still do it. But maybe not every single day.

Avoid the temptation to penny-pinch on everything and end up miserable (and probably alone as nobody likes a cheapskate).

Can You Choose A Cheaper Alternative?

When it comes to monthly fees or stuff you pay out for on a regular basis, you need to consider if you really need that specific thing.

Rather than shopping from the 'finest' range for all your food, could you buy a different brand? Could you really tell that much of a difference? I can't, but then I can't cook for shit so that's not saying much.

Do you really need to buy the most expensive bottle of wine on the shelf or can you get a cheaper one that tastes nice and still has the same benefits (i.e. getting your hammered)? But do draw the line at swigging White Lightning out of a paper bag.

You may be able to stop the thing altogether. Do you really get a benefit from whatever it is you're buying repeatedly?

If you're a little bit on the fence about these things, look at pausing the payments. Then, rather than feeling like you're restricting yourself, you can see what impact not having it has on your life over the next one, three or six months. Then you can make an informed, final decision on the matter.

If you genuinely miss it and it was adding something to your life, life's too short not to spend money, so do it. But most of the time you'll probably find you don't miss it.

Personally, I'd do anything for a cheeseburger.

Another way to think of it is, 'Would I be willing to work a number of hours to pay for this?' Most people could get a job as a virtual assistant online. If you think that they might earn £15 to £20 an hour, look at something that's costing you a £100 a month, such as a Sky TV subscription.

Would you be willing to work an additional five hours every month to pay for your Sky? If you can't be arsed to work that time for it, you might not actually care that much and can sack it off.

How To Manage This Easily

If you want to get into the habit of tracking this stuff going forward – and I recommend you do – there are an awful lot of apps out there nowadays to help you.

If you go to the resources section there's a link to my current recommendations.

These apps will talk directly to your banks and credit cards to automatically track all of your spendings and help you put each thing into categories.

Now you know what to do. It's not rocket science. It might be uncomfortable, but it's now time to just do it.

CLOSE

If your income is less or equal to your outgoings, you need to keep repeating these two chapters until you're a better human.

You're not allowed to move onto Basic Principle #3 until your income is higher than your outgoings. That's right. I'm prohibiting you from enjoying any more of my riveting financial advice until you've done this step successfully.

This hurts me almost as much it pleases you.

Whether that means increasing your incomings or decreasing your outgoings, I don't care. Just make sure your income is higher than your outgoings.

If incomings and outgoings are more or less the same, now is the time you need to put on your big boy pants, and to tighten your belt, and get a bit of wiggle room in there.

Maybe you have to swap to a cheaper alternative or cancel something altogether. But you need to have a cold, hard look at where your money is going and where you can improve.

BASIC PRINCIPLE #3
GETTING TO GRIPS WITH YOUR ASSETS

An asset is something that adds money to your pocket rather than taking it away. Another definition could be that it's something that appreciates in value over time.

In an ideal world, you want your assets to create enough income each month to pay you what you need to live on.

In the past, most people's main asset was the pension they were building up. Nowadays pension values have been eroded massively and it's basically because people are living too long. We just won't die. How selfish!

"FUN FACTS"

In 1949 the average life expectancy was 67.8 years, but those lucky enough to reach 65 years old could then expect to last another 13.1 years.

Fast forward to 2009 and the average life expectancy was 80.1 years. And if you hit 65 you'll probably kick around for another 19.3 years. (Source: Office for National Statistics)

I have every intention of living to 118 so I can see in the New Year in 2100. Then on 1st January 2100 at 00:04 my last words will be – "New Years in 2000 was better."

The other big asset that people had was their own home. This was the general plan:

- Buy and move up the housing ladder as far and as fast as you can
- Hope that it appreciates in value, but it doesn't actually produce any money for you on a day-to-day basis. I mean, you try buying some bread with a south-facing garden.
- Then, at some point in the future when you retire, downsize and sell your mansion or whatever level you managed to get up to and swap that for a shitty little static caravan somewhere. Use the money left over to buy a pension and be able to afford non-brand beans on toast.

Now call me weird, but that doesn't sound like the greatest plan in the world. It seems a little bit depressing, so what are the alternatives?

Good assets put money into your pocket each month, so a rental property would be a good example of a good asset. It can produce a rental income for you, so it's generating cash each month and when you come to sell it the hope is (fingers crossed) that it's gone up in value over time.

Another asset is owning shares in a business. This could be one you've set up yourself, in which case that's probably going to be one of the best ROIs (return on investments) you can get. Or you can buy into somebody else's company and get a portion of their profit.

You can also lend money out and get interest back for letting somebody else use it, or you can buy things like collectibles and other desirable things. Things like gold Sierra Cosworths, but we'll cover in more detail later when we talk about commodities and alternative investments.

What's important is that you pick something that's going to work for you over the long term. There's no point trying to jump from shiny object to shiny object. You need to recognise when an asset is going to work for you.

Assets that don't pay out a positive cash flow could be more of a capital appreciation play (i.e. you hope you buy low and can sell high).

Some things will only give you a benefit when you sell. Other things are going to be a mix of the two, so they'll pay out on a regular basis and hopefully go up in value.

Using a tenanted property as an example, when the tenant moves out you still have to pay any mortgage you might have on it, so it stops putting money into your pocket and actually starts taking money out. But over the long run, it will be putting money in and probably going up in value at the same time.

People who are worth less than £2-5million should really focus on cash generation. You need assets that are going to be cash-flow positive each month.

When you start getting to a higher level of net worth, that's when you can focus more on capital appreciation, because you can afford to buy and hold rather than relying on the regular income.

At this point, you might be a little bit miffed and assume you don't have any assets already, but there's a good chance you do.

- Savings accounts
- Cash ISA
- Stocks and share ISA
- Those four shares in BT that your nan gave you in 1983
- £25 worth of Premium Bonds that somehow you own and you're not quite sure where they came from.
- Swear jar money in a biscuit tin in the kitchen that you're using to save up for holiday
- The family silver that turns out once belonged to the Queen's nan's uncle's dog walker's sister-in-law. So is probably worth a mint!

Review your potential assets and tot these up in the assets column of the resource sheet.

BASIC PRINCIPLE #4
LIMIT YOUR LIABILITIES

We're not talking about your mate Dave who always seems to get into a fight on a night out. What we're looking at here is the stuff that costs you money or is dropping in value.

This will be things like your Xbox, a holiday home in the Lake District that you never use, a car, the mortgage on your house, credit card debt, etc.

HOW TO MEASURE YOUR LIABILITIES

Go back to your outgoings and the things that you're paying for on a regular basis. Look at which ones are paying for a debt.

Is it a mortgage payment, car payment, credit cards, contracts for phones, broadband, TVs, and things like that? Basically, anything that will lead to someone popping round to break your knees if you stop paying.

If so, be a dear and stick it on the list of liabilities in the spreadsheet.

You need to get the balance right between your assets and liabilities. This is going to give you what's known as your "net worth" and the goal is for your assets-to-liability ratio to be positive.

When people refer to Bill Gates as being rather well off, the number that they quote is his net worth. That means his assets minus his liabilities gives the number they say he is worth.

What you want to do is turn your total net worth into something that is providing you with an income. You want something that is going to give you your, 'Screw you work, I am done with you' in-comings figure.

Net Assets	Return	Monthly Income
£ 900,000.00	4.00%	£ 3,000.00
£ 720,000.00	5.00%	£ 3,000.00
£ 600,000.00	6.00%	£ 3,000.00
£ 514,285.71	7.00%	£ 3,000.00
£ 450,000.00	8.00%	£ 3,000.00

Figure 1 How much you need in assets if your target is £3,000 per month and you achieve the stated return.

From the table above you may realise that you do not have enough assets available currently to pay for your Screw You Income.

But showing you how to convert your surplus income into assets that provide an income is the goal of this book.

Sadly, you can't just do a runner when the going gets tough. Look at that guy John Darwin, who vanished when he was out canoeing. He faked his own death so he and his wife could get the life insurance pay-out to "sort out" their financial woes.

Didn't quite work out in the end though, did it? It's a little extreme to have to take up canoeing just to balance the books. I hate water and I can't swim. That isn't the only reason I really don't like this "fake your own death" plan though.

When you go through your figures, you need to categorise your payments into good and bad liabilities and, usually, that means what it's attached to.

For example, a good liability or good debt is something that you're using to own an asset that generates you cash. It's the "speculate to accumulate" thing.

I know I keep using it, but a good example is a buy-to-let property. You're going to have a mortgage on that, so that's a liability, but if it's a good property that you rent out and it brings more in than it costs you in the mortgage, that's not a bad thing.

Similarly, if you're an entrepreneur and you've got all of your systems nailed, taking a loan out to invest in Facebook ads to grow your customer base could be a good liability to have.

Having a Rolls-Royce as your family run-around and using it to pick up the kids from the roller disco is probably not ideal. That's a bit of a liability.

But that exact same car used for hiring out for premium weddings suddenly makes the debt you're in to own that car a good one.

Different degrees of consideration come into play when looking at these liabilities, whether good or bad.

An obvious bad one is a general car. It's likely to go down in value when you own it and there will be expenses involved maintaining it. If you have a real old banger and things keep falling off, you will have to pay out money on a regular basis to fix it.

Having said that, you also have to remember the human cost and the benefit involved.

You may see your phone contract as being a bad liability because – let's face it – a two-year-old iPhone is not worth as much as a brand spanking new one.

But is the ability to connect and interact with the outside world worth £20, £30, £40 a month to you?

Probably a yes, but I suppose it depends who your friends are.

You really need to assess what everything is worth to you. There's no judgement here. If you'd rather take out a loan and go on holiday for two weeks and not have a car, then that's cool.

If you want to spend £200 a month on prostitutes as that's what floats your boat, then happy days. Crack on. All I'm asking is you have some financial prudence, that you behave responsibly and that you pay the hookers with cash rather than credit cards.

And just as long as this comes after your essential expenditure pot and your savings pot have been topped up first.

BASIC PRINCIPLE #5
WHERE ARE YOU GOING?

Your mission, if you choose to accept it, is to get your assets large enough that they cover the cost of the liabilities you have attached to them each month and also your outgoings. There's a reason I'm a finance guy and not a writer for Hollywood blockbusters.

However, this mission is going to give you Screw You Money.

Yay!

But first, you're going to need to calculate the number you need to cover your expenses. There are three levels to doing this.

Basic Income Figure

The first level aims to replace your basic income and cover all of your essential spending. That's things you need for the no-frills, bare minimum lifestyle. Basically, it's the food in your belly and licence for your telly.

Isn't that a song?

And a house to live in. They're the essentials. This number will give you the confidence to know that if you can't or won't work again, you're at least not going to find yourself homeless and starving. That's the very first level.

Fun Income Figure

The second level is more of a full income replacement. This is going to give you a fun life, but it's not going to be all you've ever wished for and more. You'll have some treats in there, but you might have to make some compromises along the way.

You might downgrade your car and you might not have as many holidays as you'd like but, equally, you don't have to work if you don't want to. So, you know, swings and roundabouts.

Dream Income Figure

The third target figure is your ideal income. This is the fun one!

How many holidays a year would you like? How much would you like to spend on the perfect car, and what's the rent on the house you'd like to live in? What are the costs involved in spending most of your time doing that random hobby you love so much?

Really go through line by line everything you'd like to own, to have and to do, and work out the monthly or annual cost for that.

That total is your Dream Income Figure.

Here's some more maths for you. To figure out what your Net Asset Value needs to be in order to achieve those goals, we need to work backwards from the income they will produce.

A few examples are modelled in the table below. It shows how much you need to have invested at various interest rates to give you £1,000 per month income.

Interest rate	Cost per £1k per month	Multiply target figure by this figure to calculate required investment amount
4%	£300,000	300
5%	£240,000	240
7%	£171,500	171.5
10%	£120,000	120
12%	£100,000	100
15%	£80,000	80
20%	£60,000	60

Table 1 Multiply your target income by the figure in the right depending on what interest rate you can receive.

So let's say your Dream Income Figure is £10,000. You would need anywhere from £600,000 to £3million.

Bit of a wide range isn't it?

If your Fun Income Figure is £2,713 and you are confident of achieving 7% a year return then 2713 x 171.5 = £465,280.

Knowing the kind of return you can achieve from the various asset classes is what we'll look at in the next section.

The obvious is true – the lower the return, the lower the risk. However, returns of 12 per cent or more, while not easy by any stretch of the imagination, are achievable by most people with a sensible, thought-out, long-term investing strategy.

Now that you know how to generate some extra money and spend a little bit less of it, we should look at how you can start sensibly investing and allocating those funds to get you closer to the Net Asset Worth you need.

Close

You now know how to look at your incomings and whether that's something you can increase and if you want to dedicate time to it.

You have looked at your outgoings and you know exactly what you're spending your money on and why. You're also having a genuine, heartfelt chat with yourself to see whether you should be paying for this shit still or not.

You've looked at your assets and things you own that are worth something. You've also identified the liabilities and whether they're any good at helping you reach your income goals.

And, finally, we've figured out the numbers you need to be aiming for both as a monthly income and as a net worth.

Quiz

1. You decide you need to earn a bit more money, so you check your incomings over the last 12 months. Which one of the below should you probably focus on repeating this year?
   a) Wedding money
   b) Winning on the Grand National
   c) Teaching a short course on 'How to Build Rockets from Toilet Rolls'

2. Reviewing your outgoings, you've come across a few items. Decide whether they should be kept, ditched or reduced.
   a) Electricity for your home
   b) 300mb broadband
   c) Personalised wake-up call from Jessica Alba every day
   d) Toothpaste
   e) Weekly manicures

3. Which of these is an asset and which is a liability
   a) Car loan
   b) Car loan (you're an Uber driver)
   c) Credit card debt
   d) 1st Class stamp from 1812
   e) Discarded bubble gum
   f) Discarded bubble gum from Elvis Presley
   g) Vodafone shares
   h) Carillion shares

SECTION 3

ASSET

CLASSES

"Money is something you have to make
in case you don't die"

Max Asnas

There are various types of assets and we are going to look at each one in turn in this section.

You will learn to look at how risky they are, what returns you might expect, and how you can pull it all together to build yourself a balanced and sensible portfolio.

If you've forgotten already what an asset is, go back and read the previous chapter again. If you've skipped straight to this section, stop cheating.

Bad skipper. Bad.

ASSET CLASS #1
EQUITIES/SHARES

Equities (or stocks or shares) represent part ownership of a single company. You can vote on how the business is run and, more importantly, receive a share of the profits that the company makes each year via a dividend payment.

If you pretend to be a grown-up and listen to the news, you'll hear financial commentary on the Footsie (FTSE), the S&P 500, the Dow Jones, the Nasdaq, DAX, Nikkei (Check the glossary for what these stand for – for funsies). But these are all just groups of equities.

When they say the FTSE is up, this means the share prices of the companies that make up the FTSE have mostly gone up.

PROS OF EQUITIES/SHARES

- The world is capitalist so pretty much everything we do, own, use, want, need and hate is provided to us by a business. You can participate in the growth of most of these businesses via the stock market.
- They're cheap to trade.
- If you pick well, you can potentially have high dividends or achieve very high growth. You tend not to be able to get both, though.
- It gives you exposure to most types of businesses globally and there's potential to make huge returns. For example; if you wanted to invest in Bitcoin but thought it was a bit

complicated and dodgy, you could invest in the company that produces the technology that is used by the crypto community for mining. Nvidia is one of the biggest players in that industry and its share price has gone from $12 to $220 in the last five years (Source: NASDAQ: NVDA, Jan 2013 – Jan 2018)

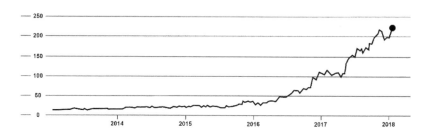

Cons Of Equities/Shares

- Equities can be very volatile. They're not the most volatile asset class we'll look at, but they're right up there. Worst case scenario, the company goes bust and you lose everything.
- The fact that you get to vote on how the company is managed is seldom used by most people. And even if you do, nobody really gives a shit.
- You don't have enough sway to have any influence on the direction of the company.
- There are thousands of individual companies you can invest in so knowing which one to pick is very hard and time-consuming. It's usually the full-time job of a bunch of people to try and select the right equities to buy – and they often balls it up anyway.

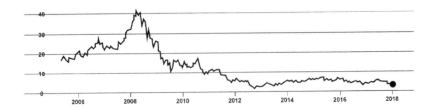

The above shows the share price of Nokia. Remember them? Not really that big of a deal anymore are they?

This share fell out of favour and they lost a lot of market share in the mobile phone market. The price went from €40 in October 2007 down to €4 in January 2018.

Back in the day, everyone had a Nokia. If you were buying shares at the time, you'd probably have thought this would be a good one to own. Alas, their market dominance was no way near as indestructible as their flagship product, the Nokia 3210.

RISK/REWARD RATIO

Equities are very volatile and it's quite hard to pick a winner. Your worst outcome is a 100 per cent loss, but your upside is virtually un-limited. In reality, though, you'll probably be looking at a return of five to 12 per cent per year over the long term.

There are two ways to decide on how to pick a company to invest in. You can look at it on either a fundamental or technical basis.

Fundamental analysis looks at things such as the story behind the company. Are they entering a new market? Do they have a new product? Are the people managing the company very good? Fundamentally, are this company, this industry and this business going to do well into the future? The downside to that, though, is you might buy a very good company but pay too much money for the shares.

The way to avoid doing that is by using something called technical analysis, which is looking at price charts and price action. Price action is how it's performed over the last few days, weeks, months or years. Technical analysis is the real numbery, geeky stuff. This is what day traders tend to be heavily into.

The best way to pick your stocks is by combining both approaches. A lot of people are either firmly in fundamental or the technical camps and don't see the worth of the other.

But if you combine the two, you can use the fundamental analysis to select companies you believe in and who have an interesting potential future, and then use the price charts to see if you're paying the right price for it.

You can buy a good company but pay too much and get screwed. Or buy a bad company but pay so little that you end up doing quite well out of it.

TIME HORIZON FOR EQUITIES

Equities are a long-term investment and so you're looking at decades, if not longer, in which you must keep your hat in the ring.

There's a saying: "It's not about timing the market, it's about time in the market." This basically means that the longer you can stay invested, the better your chances of doing well with equities.

You can trade in and out on a daily basis, but that would make you a day trader and that is beyond the scope of this book.

And honestly, most people who day trade lose money. Unless you're some kind of financial masochist, I suggest you avoid it.

BARE MINIMUM COMMITMENT

Equities are relatively cheap and easy to buy, but there are trading fees each time you buy or sell something. Keep that in mind when deciding how much to invest.

Generally, the minimum amount to invest will be £500 as a lump sum or £50 per month. That way the fees of £5 to £10 won't completely rob you of your money. Automatic monthly investing tends to be much cheaper.

ASSET CLASS #2
FUNDS

A fund is a broad term that covers a multitude of investments, but they basically allow you to own a little bit of a lot of things.

If it's an equity fund, then it gives you a basket of various shares that should give you some diversification and reduce your risk.

Equity funds can be split up into different flavours. For example, it could be by the market, by the sector, themed or different combinations. It could be geographic, so you could buy a fund that covers just the UK – a FTSE 100 fund perhaps.

Equally, you could buy a European fund or BRIC (Brazil, Russia, India, China) fund.

If you buy by thematics you could have utilities, pharmaceutical or mining companies; anything like that.

The other way to split equity funds is by their management. Some are actively managed and involve a manager, who looks after the fund and the selection of shares that are bought.

And then there is a tracker fund, which is very straightforward as it follows a basket of goods on a mathematical basis. There's less opportunity for people to pick something and get it wrong, and it just tracks the underlying asset class.

Pros Of Funds

- Lower volatility (yay!) because you're spreading your risk across not just one individual share, but a number of them

- You're paying an expert a fee so you get access to their skills and research team, which is able to dig out opportunities you may not know about or be able to get access to

- You can cover the entire globe with what you're buying, so you can get access to anything you can think of without having to pick individual shares or have accounts in random countries

- Less research is needed compared to individual shares. You do not have to go through a bazillion different companies and figure out which is the best share for you, which is most likely to go up and which one pays the biggest fees. Instead, you look at the hundreds of funds, look at their past performance and see if what they're offering is the right fit for you. But don't forget their fees!

- Trackers are a basket of things – usually shares – that track the underlying asset. There's no manager involved, so they tend to come with much lower fees. Historically, the performance of these has outperformed actively managed funds, which has seen them grow in popularity over the last few years.

Cons Of Funds

- Because there is diversification, you're not only lowering the volatility, but you're also lowering your potential gains. If you own a fund containing 100 companies and one of them doubles in price, you've made a one per cent gain instead of 100 per cent if you owned that share directly

- Fees can eat into the compounding benefits, significantly. So when we were talking about compounding before; the initial payments, the annual management fees, the exit fees, all of these costs can massively eat it into your long-term performance, so you really need to keep an eye on the fees when you're assessing a fund.

- A tracker fund might not be as diversified as you think. A tracker of the FTSE 100, might seem like a good spread of risk across the top hundred companies in the UK.
The reality is you're heavily weighted in the top 10 or 20 biggest companies in that market. In the FTSE, that means you're overweight in banking, mining, oil and pharmaceuticals. Might not be a bad thing, but something you need to be aware of

- Although funds tend to follow the price performance of the underlying asset, there is also a human element involved. Funds can become popular or unpopular and one of the big reasons why a fund might tank in price is if there's a change of fund manager. If someone's been very successful for a very long period of time and they leave the job, people might pull out their money from the fund.

Risk/Reward Ratio

They are less volatile than direct ownership of an asset as they spread the risk across a number of different things. So, the risk to reward ratio is heavily influenced by what the underlying asset is.

For example, the dotcom crash and the 2008 crash had significant impacts on funds that were invested in equities.

You are much less likely to see a fund drop to zero per cent in value compared to a company. It would be very unfortunate for that to happen, but it can in theory.

On the other hand, the likelihood of a 10,000 per cent gain is unlikely in the short or medium term.

You should be targeting a return of around five to 10 per cent per year over the long term, but with smaller swings up and down compared to equities.

Time Horizon For Funds

As most funds invest in equities, then the same time horizon counts here. Think in terms of years and decades.

Bare Minimum Commitment

A £500 lump sum investment and £50 per month on a regular payment basis should be enough to get you started.

ASSET CLASS #3
Bonds

Bonds are really just IOUs. You are lending money to somebody and tying up your cash in return for a monthly or annual interest payment.

The rate of return you get is generally proportional to the stability of the organisation asking for the money off you in the first place. That's based on how risky the other person is.

A way to think about the differentiation between the returns is covered in the following example.

Think of the US government as being your rich uncle and he asks to borrow £10 to buy a round of drinks at the pub. You know you're probably going to get that back and you don't have to worry about that too much, so you're not going to ask him for much more than your £10 back when you get home.

Junk bonds, on the other hand, are like some random bloke you just bumped into down the pub asking to borrow £100 because he's got a great business idea. You probably shouldn't lend him the money, but if you do you are going to want a lot back in return to pay for the risk of him not paying you back.

The risk to each counterparty is measured by several companies, but the big ones are Standard & Poor's and Moody's.

Pros Of Bonds

- Bonds tend to be much less volatile than either funds or equities and they're a good store of wealth
- They give a consistent return over time
- They give you guaranteed results if the issuing company and organisation still exists at the end of the term
- They've been around for hundreds of years because the issuance of debt is pretty much the backbone of capitalism

Cons Of Bonds

- They can give very, very low return on investments. The returns from some companies and countries have been low for a very long period of time. Japan has a goal of keeping its bond yield (the amount of money it pays out to bondholders) at zero per cent. So you lend them money for ten years and they just give you the same back after a decade. No interest. It's been like that since the 1980s
- The growth in the price of bonds is generally quite low. You're unlikely to get stellar performance, so you will buy at a certain return and it's unlikely to change hugely while you hold it
- There is a risk of potential losses if you don't hold the product until it is redeemed. If you are forced to sell, you might have to do so at a time when the bonds are not popular and, therefore, are worth less than you paid

- There's also the counterparty risk here that the people issuing the bonds might go bust and may not be able to pay back the debt anymore

RISK/REWARD RATIO

They're lower risk, provided that you avoid the junk bonds. You can potentially lose your initial investments and stop getting your payments if the company or government collapses.

Typically, the returns you'll be looking at for a stable Government or very secure company issued bond will be one to four per cent.

Higher than four per cent interest will be paid by trustworthy companies (the big ones that you've heard of) and slightly sketchier governments.

Above eight per cent interest is junk bond territory or countries that may decide not to bother paying back their debts.

TIME HORIZON FOR BONDS

Five years is about the shortest you want to go, but there are some countries – Austria, for example – that recently issued a 100-year bond. There are also some indefinite, open-ended bonds out there that are usually issued by governments or some larger companies.

For most individual investing, you'd be looking at five to 50 years in length.

Bare Minimum Commitment

For funds, £100 per month. If you're going to buy the bond direct from the company then you're probably looking at more like a £5,000 lump sum.

ASSET CLASS #4
CURRENCIES

Currencies aren't really an asset class, but it's potentially an asset you might have. It's all that foreign money you've got left over from your holibobs.

But you can invest in currencies. You can buy dollars with your pounds and you can trade the difference between the two.

I have only included this "asset class" in the book because people are often sold on the idea of being a foreign exchange trader, so I wanted it for completeness. Short answer – don't do it. You'll probably lose money.

PROS OF CURRENCY

- It is a very, very liquid market. You can trade it five-and-a-half days a week, 24 hours a day
- It's very good for trading and short-term investing, but less so for buy and hold investing
- In theory, it shouldn't go to absolute zero, but if you buy a currency that goes through hyperinflation it near enough could.
- Worst case, you can always go to the country on holiday and spend it. I said "worst case". Don't get any ideas, you crafty spendthrift, you!

Cons Of Currency

- It's very fast moving so there's much less time to do your due diligence
- High-frequency traders will be in and out of trades in fractions of seconds. They even go to the extent of knocking buildings down to get new internet connections made just to be able to improve their speed by seconds
- A lot of trades are done by bots, so it's hard to compete with them from a speed point of view
- It's not really what you should be doing. This isn't really investing for the long term. It's effectively a job. It could be a part-time job, but it is still a job. And you don't really want to be doing that if you're looking to have a degree of freedom in the future.

Risk/Reward Ratio

It's very easy to lose all of your money very quickly because most currency trades are leveraged.

If you get it right, probably from blind luck, then you could make huge sums of money very quickly. That's why the advertisers of courses on currency trading have a good story to tell.

If you are willing to spend several months, if not years, learning and practising then, yeah, it's a thing.

You can't hear the intonation of my voice, which reached peak sarcasm in the last sentence. To remove any ambiguity here's my opinion on currency trading – don't.

Time Horizon For Currencies

From an investing perspective, seconds to weeks are the timeframes involved.

From a time spent learning how to not fuck it all up and lose your money quicker than it takes to read this sentence, it would be 12 to 18 months.

Bare Minimum Commitment

This isn't for the faint-hearted and you're probably looking at £2,000 up front.

Remember, this is a job. It's not something you can set up and forget. It will be a time-suck.

The biggest, most important takeaway from this section is that if you are going to trade currencies, you need to have a lot more information than is available in this book.

Have I made you suitably terrified of currency trading? If so, fantastic. Stay fearful.

ASSET CLASS #5
Commodities

Commodities are basically stuff and things that tend to be used in commercial or industrial processes. So, shit like:

- oil
- gold
- oranges
- cadmium
- pork bellies
- platinum
- silver
- wheat

...and other stuff you can use and eat.

You're buying it because it has a practical use, either now or in the future. And you are speculating on the industrial production growing over time, which means us making and consuming more stuff. That's a pretty safe bet given that it is what we've done since the beginning of humanity.

As demand for something increases, the resources that make the thing get more and more scarce and the higher demand results in an increase in prices.

For example, the total amount of gold in the world has been calculated. We know what has already been mined and what is still in the ground. That supply is not changing, so if demand increases for gold then the prices go up. Until alchemy becomes a thing, it's probably a safe bet that gold is going to go up in price over time.

Pros Of Commodities

- It's a real, tangible thing that isn't tied to money, but instead to value. Using gold as an example, one ounce of the stuff in Roman times would allow you to buy a fly AF toga. If you fast forward several hundred years into the mediaeval era, that same ounce of gold would have bought you a suit of armour, also pretty pimpin'. Fast forward again to now and an ounce of gold is going to get you a fancy-pants James Bond-esque Savile Row suit.

  Over time, over thousands of years, you've been able to buy the same thing for one ounce of gold. The actual monetary value changed massively, but the value that's stored in gold hasn't. That's kind of important.

- As humans, we tend to get more productive as we go on and this causes inflation. As we get more productive, we start making more stuff and stuff is made of things.
(I told you this asset investment lark was dead easy). Think about what goes into the production of a phone and the raw materials needed. The more people there are, the more phones will be manufactured and the more demand there will be for the raw materials. As the raw materials become rarer, they become more expensive and therefore the phone becomes more expensive to build. Throw in the fact the company that makes the phone wants a bit more profit and that causes inflation over time. This raises the price of your commodity stash.

- Commodities give you exposure to another market. If you think tech is going to do well then you can buy access to the raw materials that are involved in the tech industry. For example, cadmium is involved in the production of long-life batteries. So buying the commodity of cadmium is actually a long-term play on the increase in the use of solar panels, batteries, electric cars, and things like that.

- The commodity prices can signal people's thoughts on the general economic performance. When everything looks a bit dodgy, people like the safety and security of investing in commodities.

Cons Of Commodities

- The biggest con is you might just be wrong. You might get the timing completely off. Things like gold tend to be countercyclical. When the stock market is doing well, people are happy to risk their money and so they invest in the stock market. They aren't just looking at storing their value in gold. If you happen to buy at the wrong time, you can find gold going down in price.

- It's quite difficult to liquidate when you might want to. If you have invested in the materials that go into house building and you try to sell during a massive housing crash, then you might struggle to get the best price.

- Commodities, generally, are a great way of storing your wealth, but not to grow your wealth. So that ounce of gold you held when you were a Roman still only buys you a suit. It's not turned you into someone who owns several flashy suits.

- One of the other risks is that the commodity itself becomes replaced. Asbestos, for example, used to be used in a lot of things. Then awareness of associated health issues arose and that meant we no longer wanted it and demand dropped massively. That's a historic example but a potential future victim could be oil. It is in limited supply and so scientists are looking at replacing it as soon as possible. When that happens, and we no longer need to use oil, then the demand for that will drop hugely and so will the price.

RISK/REWARD RATIO

They're relatively low-risk because, fundamentally, we'll always be eating something and we're always going to have to buy stuff and things. And we now know that commodities are the things that makes the stuffs. So, it's less likely to completely tank but, equally, it's less likely to massively rocket up in value and there's always the element of storing value.

There generally isn't a yield on commodities, i.e. they don't pay out money on a regular basis. The return is limited to changes in prices.

In the last 10 years, wheat has been as low as $2.45 per bushel and as high as $10.34 per bushel.

Disclaimer: I had no idea what a bushel was until I googled it. Now that I have, I'm still not sure. But it's a unit anyway.

TIME HORIZON FOR COMMODITIES

As long as you want to hold it for. The aim is to keep it forever and a day, because most commodities will outlast you (except the ones you eat, but please don't eat 40-year-old pork. It doesn't taste better with age. Yet again, I provide you with more nuggets of wisdom outside my main area of expertise. You're most welcome).

BARE MINIMUM COMMITMENT

You're probably looking at £100 a month for either a fund that covers the commodity or as a direct investment.

ASSET CLASS #6
PROPERTIES

Property investment covers a fair few different types of investment. Residential properties are what you live in, commercial properties are the places you work from, industrial are places where stuff is made and land is the thing you're sitting or standing on.

There are then different ways of owning property. You can buy a property directly or you can do it indirectly by buying shares or funds in property companies (referred to as Real Estate Investment Trusts - REITs).

Another way of owning property is via a joint venture with other people, so it's shared but not necessarily shared with thousands of people through a fund.

PROS OF PROPERTY INVESTMENT

- It is tangible and not a financial instrument. There are literally bricks and mortar behind the investment
- It has a proper real-world utility as people will always need somewhere to live and work. Even when all our jobs are replaced by robots, the robots are still going to need a shed to work out of
- Somebody needs to own that land and own that building that the robots work in. Hopefully, it won't be a robot that owns it

- They're relatively stable investments from a price perspective. That's because a lot of the price of a property is held within the land itself and we're not really building that much more land, as Mark Twain told us. Having said that, if you own land next to Fukushima or Chernobyl then there's the potential that it will be worth absolutely nothing. But if you own a house there that might be the last of your worries
- The returns on property are relatively consistent over time. You can pick a rate of return that fits your level of risk. If you buy a property that is rented out to Tesco for 25 years, that's pretty low risk and the return you'd get is going to be fairly low. If you rent to an independent corner shop then the risk of default is higher and therefore the return should be higher
- The biggest pro of property investment is it's what rich people do. They tend to be quite good at keeping hold of their money and taking money from other people, so if they do it there's an argument that you should as well. If you think of companies like McDonald's, they're less of a burger company and more of a property investment company, because they own the sites that the McDonald's franchises operate from
- Over time, property tends to out-strip inflation with its growth, which is always nice
- You get to use someone else's money to buy yourself an asset. This is called leverage. You go to a bank and ask for money to buy a property. You then you ask somebody else (tenant) to pay that debt off for you. If the property prices

continue to go up, you get to make a profit on the rent as well as owning an asset that is being paid for by your tenant

- Indirect investment through REITs gives you the opportunity to invest in a larger group of properties, international markets or much more expensive property. You can pool your resources so you own part of Canary Wharf instead of just a two-bed terrace. The fun part of a REIT is somebody else is doing all of the work with the tenants and the property itself

- REITs allow for a lot of diversification. If you want to buy industrial units that are used for distribution centres, that's probably easier to do as a fund than it is to try and buy a warehouse at the end of the M6

Cons Of Property Investment

- It's pissing expensive to get into on your own. Residential property is generally more accessible for individuals, but if you only have £20,000 to £30,000 then investing in a single property is going to be all of your money in one asset, which might be a little bit too risky. Commercial property is generally more expensive. Land, for anything reasonable, you're talking into the hundreds of thousands and then for big commercial stuff like office blocks it can run into the hundreds of millions.

- Property investing usually comes tied to a liability. The leverage and using other people's money that was a "pro" only a few minutes ago is also a "con". Fickle aren't I? If you don't have a tenant and nobody is paying you money, you still have to pay the mortgage. There's also the maintenance liability and the insurance that goes with a property. You have to make sure the building is still going to stand up or your tenants might not be happy. At times, you do have to do some work. It's definitely not as passive if it's directly owned.

- If it is indirectly owned via a REIT then that issue doesn't exist (for you personally). If you do go for the hands-off root and pass the problem over to somebody else, it can go pear-shaped if the people managing it screw it all up. So the management team is an important criterion for REITs.

- While a REIT can be quickly and easily bought, there can be issues with selling your share of the fund during a crash. Direct property investment takes ages to buy and sell, so you have to keep that in mind when you're looking at the investment timeframe.

RISK/REWARD RATIO

If you invest sensibly, it's hard to go wrong with property. The problem is, too many people think it's easy and anyone can do it. They're wrong.

It's very unlikely that your investment will drop to £0, so there is downside protection. If the place burns down, you should have insurance to pay out. If the building blows away and you don't have insurance, well, you should still own the land so that has a value.

The returns you can expect will vary wildly. REITs are going to be returning around three to five per cent per year, while direct investment should give you a return on the money you put into the property of anywhere from four to 12 per cent without too much difficulty.

It's a book in itself to go through all the various options, but this should give you a nod in the right direction.

Time Horizon For Properties

You're looking at 20 years, ideally, to give yourself the chance to go through a full property cycle. But the longer the better when it comes to property investment.

Bare Minimum Commitment

If you're going to invest through indirect funds and REITS, then it can be as low as £100 a month.

If you're going to be investing directly in property, you're looking at a minimum of £20,000 really – that's £15,000 deposit and £5,000 in fees.

ASSET CLASS #7
CASH

Cash is simply the currency that you use in the country that you're currently in. It's also the number in your bank account when you go online and the physical notes and coins you carry around.

It's the shit you use to pay for stuff and it's a good way of transferring value.

Without going too far into a history of money, we used to barter with people. "I'll give you a leg of the deer I just caught in return for you giving me somewhere to stay for the night in your cave."

Money came about because it was much easier to walk around with than carrying a goat while looking for some bloke who wants to trade that for a new car tyre, or something.

Money is often a reward for the time that you spend doing something, which for a lot of people are their jobs. You go to work, nine-to-five, and in return for that, you will be given some money or cash, which is nice.

PROS OF CASH

- It's really helpful for buying the little luxuries in life, like food and shelter
- You can use it to get a low-risk return. In the UK right now, it's not a great return. But the return you get tends to change throughout the cycle of the economy

- It's good to have on hand in case of an emergency. It's hard to pay for a broken window or a knackered boiler by saying you'll transfer some shares or give someone one of your bonds. They just stare at you looking baffled. It turns out that people want cash. The benefit of having cash is the fact it's immediately available to use if you need it. The fact you can get easy access to it is referred to as "liquid" in financial markets. (But that doesn't mean you're trying to put it in your smoothie).
- It's pretty safe and secure because it's backed by the Government. If you have money in a bank and the bank goes bust, the Government will pay out some of that money as part of an insurance scheme.

Cons Of Cash

- Although it's a good place to store some of your wealth, it's not going to be growing your wealth. In fact quite the opposite. When you think of the interest rate you can get, find out what the rate of inflation is. If the interest rate is lower than inflation, you're actually losing money each month. It's not making the most efficient use of your money. It's referred to as "not sweating your assets", which isn't code for a spinning class, but just means you aren't getting the best return possible
- The other downside to cash is if you've got it, there's every likelihood that you're going the spend it. It's quite easy to fritter away randomly if you've got a wallet full of cash

- Because it's physical, and the important stuff is made of paper, there is a risk of losing it or ruining it. Hands up if you have put money in the washing machine before! Hope it's not just me....

RISK/REWARD RATIO

This is very low risk indeed, but you pay for that with awful returns. You absolutely need some because, you know, that mortgage and smashed avocado on toast ain't free.

It helps you cover emergencies and gives you breathing space that will:

a) Take some pressure off and allow you to make better decisions. So if you suddenly need a new boiler and have the cash available then you can avoid freaking out about how you'll pay for it. It means you can avoid those payday loan companies with their 8,000 per cent interest rates, and you aren't forced to take a crappy price selling other assets to raise the cash

b) Allow you to buy things at the right time. All those people that buy Christmas cards in January or sunglasses in November are already taking advantage of the fact they have cash available to buy things when they are being sold off cheap

c) You can buy cheap assets when they pop up. If there's a great investment opportunity, you can use your cash to buy the asset when others might not be liquid enough to do the deal

It's good to have a cushion of maybe three to six months of your out-goings. Go back to the other chapter and see how much you spend each month. If you can have three to six months of that in cash, that's going to take a lot of pressure off.

But we don't want too much because we need to make your assets work as effectively and efficiently as possible.

TIME HORIZON FOR CASH

Cash will probably never stop being useful to have. But only on very rare occasions will you want a lot of it. It's much better to have your money working for you.

BARE MINIMUM COMMITMENT

Errrrm, £1 to open a bank account, isn't it?

ASSET CLASS #8
CRYPTOCURRENCIES

Cryptocurrencies are a brand spanking new asset class: the new kids on the block. Bitcoin is probably the most famous one and possibly the only one you've heard of.

To be honest, very few people actually understand what they are. But without going into too much depth, as it could fill an entire book on its own, it is – brace yourself – based on something called the block-chain, which is a decentralised and anonymous distributed ledger. (Are you flinching at the jargon? Sorry, I felt like showing off and using big words to look clever. My bad).

A cryptocurrency is a digital or virtual currency designed to work as a medium of exchange, using cryptography (sneaky code-breaking stuff) to secure and verify transactions. It's a database that records all of the transactions and no one can change the database unless certain specific conditions are met.

It developed because people had a general distrust of the centralised financial system. We stopped trusting governments and bankers, who were just printing money to balance the books for themselves, causing inflation and allowing massive bubbles and crashes to happen. Asshats.

It's very highly speculative and there are a mind-boggling 1400-plus alternative cryptos or AltCoins available, most of which are entirely useless. I could go on for hours about cryptocurrencies, but the honest answer is you don't really need to be concerned about it too much just yet, especially if you are early on in your investing journey.

PROS OF CRYPTOCURRENCIES

- The biggest pro for cryptocurrency right now is there are potentially huge amounts of money to be made, like a metric fuck-ton of money
- It's a brand new asset based on brand new technology that has potential (potential being the operative word) to have a huge impact on how we live our lives. It's the equivalent, if it all goes to plan, of being able to invest in the internet back in the mid-1990s. It's also, I suppose, like being able to invest in steam during the Industrial Revolution or investing in hoovers as they were first invented
- There are very small barriers to entry financially, so you can get started in cryptocurrencies with £50 (the paperwork setting up accounts is much more onerous; it makes high street banking look like a breeze)
- There are very low fees involved in buying and selling your cryptos.

CONS OF CRYPTOCURRENCIES

- The biggest con for cryptocurrency is the volatility. It's not uncommon to see 50 per cent drops in value for seemingly very little reason. For a new investor, this is usually enough to put you off for life
- You don't really know what's going on. Because there are so many new currencies available within the crypto world, the vast majority of them are not going to be around in three,

four or five years. There is a very high likelihood that anything you invest in might just disappear and you'll lose 100 per cent of your investment

- There's a very steep learning curve to get involved in this uncertain world
- If you're a technophobe, absolutely forget it. There's no chance you'll be able to go through the processes and hoops that they make you jump through to be able to invest in cryptocurrency
- There are zero regulations involved in cryptocurrencies, so there's nothing to stop anyone, particularly dodgy people, setting up fake websites, fake exchanges and generally stealing all your money off you. There's been so much hacking and general criminality around cryptocurrency that it's had a hugely damaged reputation. It's an absolute paradise for scammers
- If you forget the logins to different currencies, it is a nightmare to gain access and prove you are who you say you are. Again
- There's not enough data available and no historic trends that people can really base their trades around. The industry hasn't been around long enough for there to be any true "experts" available to teach you
- It is complete speculation and guesswork. At the time of going to press, cryptocurrency is very much a bubble, because the prices are rising and driven almost entirely by speculation without a good understanding of the fundamentals of the crypto people are investing in

Risk/Reward Ratio

Both the risk and reward are sky-high with this asset class at the moment. But with the ridiculously high-risk profile, there is the potential for very high growth as well. (Yay!).

But you could lose it all as well. (Boo!).

It's the Wild West out there, so it's the biggest financial rollercoaster that we've ever had, potentially, and this is the sort of thing that will end up in books and talked about at universities in years to come about financial crashes and bubbles.

For no other asset class have I had to repeatedly mention the high likelihood you'll be a victim of crime and you're more than likely lose a lot, if not all, of your money if you aren't careful.

Time Horizon For Cryptocurrencies

Who knows? The bubble could pop tomorrow or next year or never. These really are untested waters.

It's stupid to say "this time it's different". It isn't. It never is. But if you are going to invest in cryptocurrencies, do so at your own risk.

Be prepared to either pay attention to it a lot and be in and out within weeks, or buy for the long term and come back once a year to check on it.

Bare Minimum Commitment

Realistically looking at £100 to £200 a month, but the fees and faff of having to learn it and setting everything up mean it's probably not worth getting started unless you've got £1,000 as a lump sum.

Warning

One final note on cryptocurrencies is if you're going to invest in this asset class, you must be very comfortable with the idea that you will lose absolutely everything.

With most of the other asset classes we've discussed, there is a slim chance that you might lose everything on some of them, but the majority will – at worst – lose value, bumble along for a while, and then start to pick up again.

With cryptocurrencies, there is a much higher likelihood that they will completely disappear and you will lose everything you invested. So bear that in mind when someone is trying to sell you a get-rich-quick course on cryptocurrency trading.

ASSET CLASS #9
ALTERNATIVE

This covers pretty much everything else that you might buy that has the potential to go up in value. It can be anything. Nobody really knows what's going to become an "alternative investment".

It's something that is desired in and of itself and not for any real practical purpose. So all you people out there that have been collecting boxed, mint-condition My Little Pony toys for years, you might be quids in! Get them down the car boot sale or on eBay and get a little bit of one-off income action going on with your bank balance.

If you're more of a hands-on collector and only have a series of battered and bruised Action Men up in the loft somewhere, start looking at things like art, vintage wine collections, whisky, stamps, sporting or film memorabilia, antiques, and stuff like that.

PROS OF ALTERNATIVE INVESTMENTS

- Sounds stupid, but one of the biggest pros is just being a show-off and bit of a smug twat. I remember there was a guy who went to a whisky tasting up in Scotland and he managed to buy a supremely rare £50,000 bottle. He went out to see his friends and then intentionally dropped the whisky on the floor and smashed it. It was just to show off the fact that he could afford to buy something for £50,000 and then completely dispose of it. Then he went back and bought another one, so he could take it home and drink it. I'll give you some extra brownie points for noticing both of these purchases need to be added to the bat-shit outgoings category. I mean, that is being a show-off twat, isn't it?

- It might genuinely be a hobby of yours and could be a dream purchase, which is quite handy if it doesn't work out as an investment. For people that collect stamps because it's their hobby, happy days. It gives them something to do, keeps them out of trouble and one day, you never know, it could be worth a lot of money. If admiring your collection of vintage toys based on cartoon characters from the 1940s is your thing, cool. If it turns out to be an investment, even cooler

Cons Of Alternative Investments

- It's completely speculative
- You've got to store them somewhere safe because they are precious and will generally increase in value as they become rarer. It is going to cost you money to store them. With art, you might need a safe. With vintage wines, you might need to have a temperature-controlled warehouse. With stamps, probably don't just put them in the front drawer. You don't want to accidentally put a 200-year-old stamp on the letter to granny, do you?
- If nobody wants to buy it off you, it's entirely worthless. So even if there's one person that wants to buy it off you – unless they're entirely insane – it's probably not going to be worth that much as an investment.

Risk/Reward Ratio

It's all relative to the amount of money you spend on it. So if you're going to spend however much a stamp is nowadays, the initial start-up capital required is quite low. Equally, if you want to buy yourself a Da Vinci masterpiece, that's probably a bit more.

Time Horizon For Alternatives

It all depends on the market. If you want to buy a car that you hope will become a classic, the time frame becomes decades. What you're looking for here is for supply to become scarce over time.

That means the production of something has come to an end and people who aren't as OCD as you have been throwing out their Barbie dolls instead of keeping them in bubble wrap (raise your hand if you love popping that stuff).

From an art perspective, it sounds a bit morbid but you're waiting for the artist to die because then there's a finite supply of their work.

From a whisky point of view, the more smug twats that drop expensive bottles on the floor, the rarer it gets and that drives up the price.

For things like livestock, if you buy a thoroughbred racing horse, for instance, you kind of have to make your money while it's still alive.

Here's a tip for you. If it fucks, floats or flies then you probably shouldn't invest in it as an asset class. For the slow among you (like some of my beta-readers) think racehorses, yachts and planes.

Bare Minimum Commitment

It very much depends on what it is you're buying. And you have to think ahead and really make sure that it's in mint condition.

Having said that, you might already have some hidden treasures in your house that are in mint condition; a toy you never got around to opening perhaps? You never know, that could be an investment. Nobody knows, and you won't know for another few decades if you were right or not.

CLOSE

We've now been through all of the major asset classes that you could invest in. We've looked at equities, which are individual shares in a company. They're good if you get the right one, not so good if you make a mess of it and pick the wrong one.

You now know about funds, which give you a slightly wider spread of risk and a slightly better chance of picking the right companies because somebody else is picking them for you. But equally, you're probably going to end up with some bad ones in there as well.

We've looked at bonds that are going to allow you to lend money to other people and get a return on your money.

And then we covered currency, which unless you want to take up a new job, isn't something most people are going to want to invest in.

We've looked at commodities, which allow you to get involved in something that controls inflation.

We delved into property in some detail to look at how you can invest directly and indirectly to get exposure to that market.

We've looked at cash and the importance of having at least a buffer of three to six months' worth of expenses to take the pressure off.

And we considered the new kids on the block – cryptocurrencies. Even though it's all the rage at the moment and there's potentially a good financial reason to invest in it, there's also an awful lot of risk involved. You really should only play with speculative money on cryptocurrency.

We then looked at the alternative asset classes; random things that you probably haven't even thought of that might end up being investments. But it's quite hard to have that as an investing strategy.

Next, you will see how to put everything you've learned into action and pull together a plan. We will look at how to allocate the money you have across all these different asset classes and, once you've bought them, how to rebalance it on an ongoing basis.

QUIZ

1. Yesterday, the stock market went bat-shit crazy and lost 25 per cent of its value. Suzie laughed in the face of her colleagues because she drinks heavily during office hours, but also because she is heavily invested in which of these investments?
   a) Dungeon & Dragons figurines
   b) Bonds
   c) Cryptocurrencies

2. Which of the following is most likely to give you a heart attack watching the wild ride of price fluctuations?
   a) Funds
   b) Cryptocurrencies
   c) Property
   d) Gold

3. You've just stumbled upon a giant bin bag full of cash and have decided to invest it in a balanced and sensible way for your future. How much are you going to leave as cash?
   a) All of it. I love the smell of stolen cannabis money!
   b) £8,000 as that should cover my £2k per month expenses for a while
   c) None of it; cash is for pussies

WHAT IS ASSET ALLOCATION

Asset allocation is the way you split your money across the different asset classes and how you invest it. Ideally, you want to spread your investments across lots of different assets so that you're not going to lose it all if something shitty happens to one type.

The number one rule of investing is: Do not lose money.

The number two rule of investing is: Do not lose fucking money. It's similar to rule one, but many orders of magnitude sterner.

Now, you might be thinking, 'Why not just back the winner that's going to give me the biggest return?'

The one with the potential biggest return that we've talked about is cryptocurrency. So why shouldn't you just throw all of your money into that? Well, because that would make you an idiot.

You're not going to pick the winner every single time. And if you put all your eggs in the one basket made from TNT, there's a good chance you will lose it all.

(Interesting side note: I have a weirdly in-depth knowledge of trini-trotoluene due to my time spent at the MoD).

You need protecting from yourself. The goal is to lower the volatility and smooth out your wins and losses over time to give you the best overall return that works for you.

This is why I can't give individualised asset allocations in a book like this. All I can do is give you some pros and cons for each type of asset class and give you the information to make the decisions for yourself.

What You Need To Know

When you're looking at asset allocation, the first thing to consider is how much money you actually have to invest.

Depending on if you're broke or have £10million sitting around, the options available are quite different.

Check Your Net Worth

First things first. Once you've paid off any expensive debts (I'd count anything costing more than seven per cent a year interest as expensive) and loans, the main goal is to build your emergency fund.

This is going to help you make better decisions, as we've already covered, and give you massive peace of mind quite quickly. It also proves that you have quite a lot of financial intelligence.

The average person in the UK has a Total Net Worth of £6,200, of which only around £800 is in cash (*Source: Wealth and Assets Survey, ONS*). The fact you have a specific amount (three to six months expenses, right?) squirrelled away, puts you ahead of the majority of people in the country.

It also proves that you can manage your circumstances to live within your means and that your income is exceeding your outgoings.

Adulting achievement unlocked!

Check The Minimum Investment Criteria

Each asset class has a minimum sum you'll need to start investing. If you don't have the money, it's probably not worth worrying about it too much right now.

Check The Time Frames

Most of the assets we talked about tend to be long term. Nothing we've talked about here is a get rich quick scheme. If that's what you're looking for and you're desperate for cash now, then go stick some money on a horse and cross your fingers. This book isn't for you. Long-term, sensible investing? You're not ready for it just yet.

(Note: Don't actually put it all on a horse you dick. Re-read the first section again and grow up).

Each asset type is going to be medium to long-term relative to your age. What is long-term for someone in their 20s is probably different for what's long-term for someone in their 70s.

Generally, the longer that you can be invested the better. So time is really your friend in this case. The older you are, the less time you have to bounce back from any significant drops in your net worth. You want to start looking at moving money to less volatile assets as you start to mature.

But think of "mature" as when you'll be dead, rather than when you're going to retire.

Did you know there are around 14,500 people over the age of 100 in the UK and nearly 500,000 people over 100 worldwide?

If, on the other hand, you follow the live fast, die young philosophy then maybe you want to take a different approach to asset allocation. Lovely as it is to bankroll a donkey sanctuary into retirement, it's not much of a strategy for having a blast when you're alive!

Risk Tolerance

In the past, it was common for sharp-suited financial types to link assumptions about age to risk tolerance as part of their advice. For me – being a bit more of a maverick about finance – it has much more to do with your psychology on investing and your risk tolerances.

If you're the sort of person who, when you see your net worth tank by 20, 30 or 40 per cent, is going to panic and sell everything you've just bought at a loss and think "this isn't for me", then you need to allocate your assets to a very low-risk, low-volatility asset.

Selling when something has just dropped is probably the worst thing you could do. All you're then doing is selling when prices are low and buying back when prices are high. That's a fantastic way of losing all of your money very quickly.

If you can't handle these ups and downs mentally then you need to make a decision to pick an asset allocation that is right for you. And you must accept that you might not get the highest possible returns that others may get, but equally, you're not going to get the soul-crushing lows either.

There is no right or wrong answer. Just what's right or wrong for you.

Another element to consider is whether you have other people to look after. If you're a single person with no dependents, live in a one-bed flat, are happy to couch surf with mates and live off value digestive biscuits if you hit a lean patch, and if you died – let's be honest – nobody would really care (in financial terms only, I'd care), you can be pretty reckless.

If on the other hand you're part of a family with three or four kids, and look after your parents or your stepparents, have a couple of ponies down the stables and a Great Dane to support, then you need to be a little bit more risk tolerant and a little bit more risk-aware because you have others to consider.

Now, if you're still thinking of going all-in on something risky because you've not got that much money available and you want to go big or go home then let's do the first things first: Go and read the first section again, specifically Fundamental Principle #5.

Repeat after me: "If it looks too good to be true, you don't want to be a greedy prick. That's not going to help you. Annoying as it is, slow and steady wins the financial race most of the time."

Think about it this way, if you have £50,000 and you decide that you need a huge sum of money to retire on, would you invest into something with the potential to return 3,500 per cent within a short period of time, but only had a 2.7 per cent chance of succeeding? And that if it doesn't work out, you lose everything?

If that sounds good, go to the roulette table at your friendly local casino and put it all on your favourite lucky number 12. If it works, happy days! If you win, that's a £1,750,000 pay-out. You've just achieved your goal.

But, is it likely to happen? Really? Would you be willing to risk it all on something with such small odds of succeeding?

That's an extreme example of very high-risk asset allocation: gambling. But it's not dissimilar to putting all of your eggs into a very high-risk basket.

(Remember, there's no such thing as a f.....! 'Free lunch', I hear you say. Correct.)

So, this casino wheeze is something to think about. And by "think about", I mean completely dismiss because it's a stupid fucking idea.

Don't do it.

And don't tell anybody else about this strategy either, even if you hate them and you want to watch them get financially ruined. That makes you an awful person.

TIME TO INVEST OR LEARN

Consider how hands off do you want to be. You've got the option of being completely hands off and totally passive, but the returns that you get are going to reflect that.

Or you can get a lot more involved.

Do you want to become a professional investor?

It is an option, but would you be better served doing what you're currently doing (be that working for yourself or someone else) and continue getting paid for doing that rather than learning a new skillset, even if it might be a fun hobby?

Becoming a professional investor in any one of these asset classes is a very long-term commitment. Each asset class has the potential to become a rabbit hole to jump down to try and start learning. And remember the fund managers out there. It's their full-time job, they've done it for decades, and they still screw it up and get out-gunned in the performance stakes by the robotic trackers.

To put it into context, it's probably master's degree level studying.

Relying on your mate Barry down the pub and his recommendations isn't really great advice, either. You never know other people's motives or circumstances. The reason why I'm not giving you specific advice within this book is that I don't know everything about your circumstances.

(By the way, have you worked out all that stuff for my party you're meant to be organising for me on Saturday yet? Time's marching on).

Even if someone means well and tell you to invest in something particular, that might be perfect for them and for the person sitting next to you, but it doesn't mean it will be perfect for you.

Taking advice from strangers isn't a great idea. As for researching things on the internet? The internet is great and pretty much every human thought in the world has been put down on the internet, whether it's useful or not. You can find all the best information out there on the internet and the perfect strategy for you for free.

The problem is that you've got to wade through so much shit that you're very likely to get confused, overwhelmed and end up watching cat videos.

There's also the chance that the information will be outdated or biased. The person giving the information could be more interested in selling you something than helping you out.

So what should you do?

Find a happy balance. Learn enough to know what you're looking at and doing, but not so much you forget to actually do something because you're spending so much time researching.

Sometimes a little bit of knowledge is dangerous. In this case, it's really not.

Managing your own finances and taking responsibility for your investments is a life skill that we should be taught at school. We aren't, so I'm teaching you how right now.

What Vehicle To Invest Through

As a basic principle, you want to be investing in as tax-efficient a way as possible. In the UK that means using an ISA for most people. But I'm not an accountant or a tax adviser, so don't listen to me.

Make sure you speak to the right people when you're at the stage where tax planning becomes a thing. If you're putting away £50 a month, it's probably not too much of a worry right now.

What You Should Do

Ideally, you would invest in some low-risk assets and some high-risk assets (and some medium-risk ones just for completeness) because overall that's going to get you a reasonable rate of return over time.

If you're just starting out, then funds are probably going to be the best way to gain exposure to all the various asset classes and levels of risk in the cheapest possible way.

If, on the other hand, you've got quite a lot of money then consider investing in all the different asset classes. You baller.

Consider the fees involved and make sure you are minimising these as best you can. Also think about the time involved, both in getting set up initially and the ongoing commitment too. Is that much time required cool with you?

Finally, consider if you can cope with the plan. Are you going to be the sort of person that refreshes the screen every five minutes hoping it will go up and the result impacting disproportionately on how happy or sad you are for the day? Or are you going to be OK to leave it for three, six or 12 months, before you look and worry about it?

Is The Portfolio Asset Allocation Hands-Off Enough For You?

If it's going to be hands-on, where are you going to fill in your knowledge gaps? Do you have a plan for how you can keep up-to-date with what's going on in the assets that you just invested in? Where are you going to get the data from to help you make your decisions?

What frequency are you going to be involved in managing your investments? It may be partly based on the amount you are saving and the minimum investment.

If you save £50 a month and the minimum investment is £200 to invest – wait for it, let me do the maths.

OK. It's going to take you 418 years to save up for that lump sum.

In an ideal world, you want to be automating your investment monthly. That's going to allow you to do that pound cost averaging thing we talked about earlier.

Think about reviewing your investments on a quarterly, six-monthly or annual basis. You only need to review it on a quarterly basis at the absolute most. If you start doing it daily and weekly then you've basically become a trader – and you've got the wrong book, you spanner.

How To Choose An Asset Allocation

You can see there are lots of factors at play here. It's not hard to choose something when you know what to do, but everybody is very different.

Below are two different model portfolios. We're assuming £100,000 allocation, but which one seems more high-risk and which is low-risk?

Asset	Allocation A %	Allocation B %
Cash	5%	10%
Bonds	15%	42.5%
Equities	20%	0%
Funds	20%	25%
Property	20%	20%
Cryptocurrency	15%	2.5%
Alternatives	5%	0%

Figure 2 Guess which Asset Allocation is high risk and which is low risk.

WARNING

Do not copy these. These are both just teaching examples. Calm yourself down. You're not going to get the perfect portfolio by following either of these examples. Don't get carried away. Leave time to consider everything you've read through so far.

Let it simmer. Then, once you've decided on an allocation that's best for you, don't fuck about with it all the time. When you do review it, which is what we'll look at next is, try to avoid interfering too much.

Rebalancing Your Assets

This means assessing your winners and losers on a regular basis and moving things around to make sure things are still balanced the way you want them to be.

You're reviewing your initial allocation and the percentages you wanted for each different asset type, and then looking at your current allocation in terms of the pounds amount and the percentage amount.

When you're rebalancing and reviewing your assets, you want to consider if there is a good reason to change your target allocation.

If you're only a year into it then your asset allocation probably doesn't need to change. You change your asset allocation over the period of several years or major events. If you have a child then that might impact on your tolerance for risk and that might change your asset allocation.

Otherwise, if it is changed regularly, you're just being scared of your own shadow and moved by the market. That's not ideal.

Ask yourself, do I really need to change my asset allocation? It's a decision you shouldn't take lightly.

Asset	Target %	Actual %
Cash	10%	6.8%
Bonds	10%	7.1%
Equities	25%	23.6%
Funds	15%	16.9%
Property	20%	15.5%
Cryptocurrency	15%	28.7%
Alternatives	5%	1.4%

Figure 3 Reviewing your Asset Allocation over time to ensure you keep to your target splits.

Now, if things have appreciated a fair bit or have become undervalued, that's a trigger to think about moving money around. As you can see from the above example, because the cryptocurrency holding has increased and cash has decreased in percentage terms, it could be a good time to sell off some crypto to take profits and top up your cash holdings.

But before you pull the trigger, just check that you're not buying more of something that is now a dead duck. Even within your assets, you need to make sure you're still buying a sensible long-term investment.

Continuing to invest in that high-tech fax machine company may not be the best plan in the world.

Make sure that it's a significant enough sum of money to make it worthwhile rebalancing. If you sell £4.38 and reallocate it to bonds, well, that's a bit of a waste of time and effort. Wait until the numbers are big enough to make it worthwhile.

What You Need To Consider

Does the asset allocation still make sense for you?

Complete a full and emotion-free analysis of your asset allocation. Before you look at the numbers and how you've performed over the last three, six or 12 months, consider how it feels for you to still have that original target asset allocation.

As I've said, it's not something you should change frequently or easily or without too much thought. There must be a good reason why you want to change your asset allocation.

Being bored isn't a good enough reason.

How To Do It

You need to set some proper time aside for this; potentially a day or two. Do it with a fresh head. Schedule it in and make sure you stick to the date.

But don't do it too often either. There's no point in pissing about moving a few £100 here and there once a week. The fees are going to end up costing you more than any gain you'd get.

As we said before, make sure there's a significant enough change to make it worth doing.

Keep in mind the timeframes involved. If you're selling some shares to buy a new property, it might take a while to go through. Whereas selling funds for cash is pretty instant.

Then just plan what you're going to sell and what you're going to buy. Sell it, buy it and then leave it alone. Not rocket science is it?

CLOSING THOUGHTS

And that's about it, my friend. You've got to the end of this book, so you're officially winning at life.

The shit we're taught in school is almost entirely pointless for most of us and, unfortunately, financial intelligence isn't high on the curriculum. The fact that you've gone through this book now puts you miles ahead of most people. Well done you.

You now have the fundamentals in place. You know the importance of investing but also know that taking your time is going to work in your favour. This is the one time that being a slow git is a good thing. That's going to allow you to pound cost average and get the benefits of compounding over the long term.

You know the ropes. You know what kind of assets you can invest in, and the pros and cons of each.

When you have a chat with an independent financial adviser, rather than just being bored to tears and glazing over and praying for it to end, you can start asking them questions.

You can dig into finding out if they know a) what they're talking about and, b) what's in your best interests.

In the resource section, you will find a list of questions you can annoy any financial adviser with to make sure they know exactly what they're talking about. Would you want to go to a morbidly obese personal trainer whose job it is to get you skinny? Probably not. You need to make sure they're practising what they preach.

The most important thing though is to stop looking for a free lunch.

If it were easy, everybody would do it. Not everybody is rich. It's clearly not easy. But it is achievable for 90 per cent of the people holding this book.

There are fundamental things you need to be doing and we've just gone through them all. While I'll be the first to admit it's not the most in-depth book in every single aspect, it gives you enough of an overview for you to probably be head and shoulders above everybody else you know when it comes to finances.

If you follow the very simple rules in here, it can see you financially independent in a surprising amount of time.

Below is a simplified cheat sheet so you can check where you currently are and what you need to do next.

Let's start at the absolute bottom: Get some money. Whether that's a job, a side hustle, prostitution, your own business or bank robbery – whatever it is, start bringing in some money so that you can move up to…

The most important thing you need to do is to live within your means. I can't stress that enough. It's the keystone of everything else in this book. You need to be able to sort out your incomings and outgoings and make sure you can save each month. Then you're ready for…

You need to clear any high-interest debts that you've got. Yes, that means the bat-shit crazy payday loans and the big burly bloke down the pub who you borrowed £50 off months ago. Clearing a 29 per cent credit card debt is a guaranteed way of getting a return of 29 per cent for your investment. That's going to be hard to beat elsewhere. Once that's done, time for...

Get to grips with your circumstances, your goals, and the net worth you need to give you the income that you want in life.

Yes, it's going to be terrifying, but you need to know where you're trying to get to in the first place.

Start building up your emergency fund. Remember, buying a season ticket for some shitty football club probably isn't that important and doesn't count as an emergency. Try not to use this money for that. If you can lock it away somewhere that isn't as easy as pulling a sock drawer out then that's probably a good thing for your emergency fund.

So now you're earning, saving, have no expensive debts and have some money squirrelled away for a rainy day. Next up is...

Start investing in line with your asset allocation model. If you're doing it via an ISA, then you can be pound cost averaging in at up to £1,600 a month. That's quite a lot of money to be investing. For most people, that will probably tide you over for a fairly long time.

Once you're over that, well done you. You probably need to get more specific individualised advice at that point rather than just reading my awesome book.

Now that you're fully invested and following a strategy that puts your money into the right assets for you, you can move on to...

You get to sit and wait a while, but then it's time to start reviewing and rebalancing your portfolio.

Then just repeat until you're richer than a rich person on payday.

The timeframe from moving from this level to the next will vary massively. But once you've nailed this part, it's time to move on to...

Retire! You remember that number you set yourself as a target back at Level 4? Well, you've just achieved it! Well done, you clever little sausage.

Your assets are now of a sufficient size that they can produce an income for you that will pay for your basic/great/awesome lifestyle.

Time to enjoy the spoils of your dedicated hard work. Maybe do something stupid like spend all your money on a Fabergé egg and see if it really is an egg and if you can poach it.

Alternatively, and probably a better option, keep on top of your portfolio as this could be your full-time job. You're a professional investor, just like me.

STILL TERRIFIED?

You still might not be ready to invest just yet. Maybe you have some debts to clear or need to sort out your incomings and outgoings. You may be ready to invest, but still not 100 per cent confident to do so. What you can do for the time being is to start trading a dummy portfolio.

Give yourself an imaginary sum that is close to reality for you and use that monopoly money to pretend to invest. Split the fake moolah across the assets just as you learned in the Asset Allocation chapter.

Now watch it for the next six months to a year.

Ideally, yes, you want to start for real as soon as possible, but sprinting off in the wrong direction isn't a great idea either. Better to crawl slowly in the right direction before you get too ahead of yourself.

Invest the dummy portfolio, have a play with it and see how you get on. That might highlight some issues you've not really considered.

Finally, remember to have fun. Contrary to popular belief, life isn't short. It's actually the longest thing you'll ever do. Life is to be enjoyed, so get to it.

That's enough of all this financial bollocks. What matters is getting yourself to a position where you're comfortable and relaxed in life.

You don't want to be stressing about money or the financial future of you and your kids and your family. It's important to balance having fun now and having fun in the future.

On that note, that £1,000 that we discussed in the very first section, what would you do with it now?

If you've learned anything, I hope you'd now say something like: "Spend some of it on fun stuff cos life is awesome. But invest most of it for the future."

If you haven't paid a blind bit of notice and still want to spend it on shoes or your very own arcade machine, well, good luck to you.

So long as you're happy.

ADULTING WORDS YOU MAY NOT KNOW

ROI

Return On Investment: How much money you get back as a percentage of how much you invested.

Invest £100 and get £10 back, that's 10% ROI.

FTSE

Financial Times Stock Exchange, which is odd given it's really the London Stock Exchange.

S&P 500

Standard & Poor's 500, which is the US version of the FTSE.

NASDAQ

National Association of Securities Dealers Automated Quotations – catchy huh? Tech-focused list of 4,000-odd US companies.

Net Asset Value or NAV

This is the total of all the assets a person or company has, less all of the liabilities that person or company has.

It's a bit like equity in your house. If the house (asset) is worth £200,000 but the mortgage (liability) is £150,000. The Net Asset Value is £50,000.

Total Expense Ratio or TER

This is the measure of all the costs associated with a fund, e.g. management fees, trading fees, legal fees, etc. The total cost is then divided by the fund's total assets to give a percentage figure.

This is the figure you want to be concerned about when picking funds. If two funds are basically the same, but one has a TER of 2% versus the other having a TER of 1%, go for the 1% every time (all other things being equal).

If both of those funds returned 7% over the year, your net gain would be 5% with the first fund but 6% with the second.

I know which one I'd prefer....

Tracker / Passive Fund
A Tracker fund follows the performance of a broad market, or segment of the market. Tracker funds are sometimes referred to as Index funds.

Trackers have gained in popularity as they take out any (or most) human intelligence requirement. The fund is set up to track say the top 100 companies in the FTSE. So the fund buys a % share of every company in the FTSE 100.

That's it.

If a company falls out of the top 100, the fund sells it. Whatever company replaces it, the fund buys that.

There is no 'active' management of the fund. So no random banker deciding to buy into a company because he is mates with the Chairman.

It's "computer says no" investing.

Active Managed Fund

This is a fund that is managed by an individual, or team of people who select the investments they buy on your behalf. The vast majority of these underperform the tracker funds, but the small (very small) few who can outperform the market tend to do very well for themselves.

For most of us, these aren't worth the risk.

Gross Yield

It's when a farmer harvests disgusting vegetables.

Or alternatively, it's the percentage return you get before fees and taxes.

If you buy a bond that pays a Gross Yield of 7%, then your £100 would return you £7 per year.

There will then be fees and taxes to pay on that return, which might bring you down to £5. This then becomes the Net Yield.

Net Yield

Read what I just said above.

RESOURCES

Remember some of that stuff I said I'd give you? Well here's where you need to go to get it.

Net Asset Value worksheet

- Document your incomings, outgoings, assets and liabilities in one simple sheet
- This will allow you to identify where you can save and how much you need to invest in order to achieve financial security
- Go to www.theEPinvestor.com/book

Questions to ask your financial adviser

- Fun questions to ask that will make them squirm, and possibly cry
- Go to www.theEPinvestor.com/book

The EP Investor Podcast

- More ramblings by me about money
- Go to www.theEPinvestor.com/podcast

KEEP IN TOUCH

Need more help? Do you want to join me? Here's how.

I know this can all be a bit mind-boggling, so I thought you might appreciate a bit more moral support.

If you need to, I'm here to offer you more than just a fireside chat about investing. You lucky devil you.

Don't roll your eyes. I know it's dull, but it's easier to tough it out with friends. Trust me.

Go to www.theepinvestor.com/services to see how I can help you implement some of this stuff and help turn you into a baller.

I'd love your feedback on the book. Whether it was helpful, if it was new and breath-taking information, or if you found it all a bit boring and you knew it all before (if you got to the end of the book and knew it all, what the fuck did you pick up a general 'getting started' finance book in the first place?).

But please share your success stories with me. I'd love to hear from you. Especially with inspiring stories. I like them.

Email them to success@theepinvestor.com or post them on www.facebook.com/theepinvestor/

I genuinely believe that anyone can take the information in this book and make their financial lives 843 times better (may not have fact-checked that stat). So here's to your success.

All the cuddles

Damien Fogg

Printed in Great Britain
by Amazon